Is Islam a Religion of War or Peace?

Other books in the At Issue series:

Alternatives to Prisons
Anorexia
Antidepressants
Anti-Semitism
Are Athletes Good Role Models?
Are Chain Stores Ruining America?
Are Privacy Rights Being Violated?
Attention Deficit/Hyperactivity Disorder
Biological and Chemical Weapons
Child Labor and Sweatshops
Child Sexual Abuse
Cosmetic Surgery
Creationism Versus Evolution
Do Children Have Rights?
Does Advertising Promote Substance Abuse?
Does the Internet Benefit Society?
Does the Internet Increase the Risk of Crime?
Does the United States Need a National Health Insurance
    Policy?
Drugs and Sports
The Ethics of Abortion
The Future of the Internet
How Can the Poor Be Helped?
How Should One Cope with Death?
How Should Society Address the Needs of the Elderly?
How Should the United States Treat Prisoners in the War on
    Terror?
Indian Gaming
Is American Culture in Decline?
Is It Unpatriotic to Criticize One's Country?
Islam in America
Is Poverty a Serious Problem?
Is the Gap Between the Rich and Poor Growing?
Is There Life After Death?
Is the World Heading Toward an Energy Crisis?
Is Torture Ever Justified?
Legalizing Drugs
Managing America's Forests
Nuclear and Toxic Waste
Protecting America's Borders
Religion and Education
Space Exploration
Teen Sex
What Are the Most Serious Threats to National Security?
What Causes Addiction?
Women in Islam

At ✴ Issue

Is Islam a Religion of War or Peace?

Jann Einfeld, *Book Editor*

Bruce Glassman, *Vice President*
Bonnie Szumski, *Publisher*
Helen Cothran, *Managing Editor*

GREENHAVEN PRESS
An imprint of Thomson Gale, a part of The Thomson Corporation

THOMSON
GALE

Detroit • New York • San Francisco • San Diego • New Haven, Conn.
Waterville, Maine • London • Munich

LIBRARY OF CONGRESS CATALOGING-IN-PUBLICATION DATA

Is Islam a religion of war or peace? / Jann Einfeld, book editor.
  p. cm. — (At issue)
Includes bibliographical references and index.
ISBN 0-7377-3099-4 (lib. : alk. paper) — ISBN 0-7377-3100-1 (pbk. : alk. paper)
  1. Islam—21st century. 2. Islam and terrorism. 3. War—Religious aspects—
Islam. 4. Islam—Public opinion. I. Einfeld, Jann. II. At issue (San Diego, Calif.)
BP161.3.I7 2005
297.2'7—dc22   2004059678

Printed in the United States of America

Contents

Page

Introduction 8

1. Islam Declares Holy War on America and Its Allies 12
   Osama bin Laden

2. Many Islamic Leaders Advocate Peaceful Relations 17
   with the West
   John L. Esposito

3. Islam Is a Religion of Peace 30
   George W. Bush

4. Islam Is Not a Peaceful Religion 32
   Pat Robertson

5. Islam Promotes Terrorism 37
   Ibn Warraq

6. Islam Has Been Hijacked by Terrorists 43
   Reuven Firestone

7. The Islamic Concept of Jihad Is Comparable to the 50
   Christian Concept of Just War
   Sohail H. Hashmi

8. The Islamic Concept of Jihad Differs from the 63
   Christian Concept of Just War
   Jean Flori

9. The Muslim Prophet Muhammad Was a Gentle and 68
   Compassionate Man
   Akbar S. Ahmed

10. Muslims Must Denounce Violence Against Women 78
    Irshad Manji

11. Muslim Women Have More Rights, Respect, and 90
    Protection than Western Women
    Afsar Bano

Organizations to Contact 99

Bibliography 103

Index 106

Introduction

Islam is the second-largest and fastest-growing religion in the world. Almost one-quarter of all the world's population, or about 1.3 billion people, identify themselves as Muslims. There are fifty-five Muslim countries scattered around the globe—in the Middle East, south and southeast Asia, and Africa. A growing number of Muslims live in Europe and in the United States. With the high Muslim birthrates and the escalating number of converts, most analysts predict that some time before the middle of the twenty-first century, Islam will surpass Christianity as the world's leading religion. Some say this will happen by 2025. In response to these demographic projections, senior Islamic scholar Akbar Ahmed says, "The twenty-first century will be the century of Islam."

To many Westerners, however, this scenario may be cause for alarm. Since September 11, 2001, when Muslim suicide bombers committed the most atrocious act of terrorism against the American people in U.S. history, many people have questioned whether Islam is an inherently violent religion. Images in the Western press of Muslim terrorists beheading Americans and their supporters, bombing school buses, and slaughtering foreign tourists continue to fuel the debate about the nature of Islam. Is Islam a religion of peace that inspires people to lead lives based on justice and compassion, as President George W. Bush has claimed? Or is Islam, as Christian evangelist Jerry Falwell describes it, an extremist and violent religion?

Islam Is a Violent Religion

Christian evangelists are not alone in condemning Islam as a violent and intolerant religion. D.S. Margolieth, an eminent nineteenth-century British scholar, argued that the religion's history of violence stems from the first days of the prophet Muhammad during the seventh century. According to Margolieth, "The experiences of the Prophet's life, the constant bloodshed which marked his career at Medina [when he spread the faith in what is now modern-day Saudi Arabia], seem to

8

have impressed his followers with a profound belief in the value of bloodshed as opening the gates of Paradise." Margolieth contends that Muslim leaders have justified their murders of non-Muslims for centuries by citing Muhammad's words: "Kill the unbelievers, wherever you find them."

According to American author Robert Spencer, whose family came from the Muslim world, Islam's intolerance of nonbelievers means that the religion is not compatible with Western freedoms, liberal democracy, and human rights. He writes that Islam's "long, developed, and precisely articulated doctrine of violent jihad (holy war) against non-Muslims . . . [means] Islam is incompatible with a liberal, free, and democratic society."

Like Spencer, some human rights activists are also critical of Islam and its practices, particularly over the treatment of Muslim women and family "honor" killings. In a highly publicized case in 1999, Samia Imran, a twenty-eight-year-old Pakistani woman, sought a divorce from her violent husband after ten years of marriage. After reluctantly agreeing to meet her disapproving mother at the lawyer's office in Lahore, Pakistan (divorce is considered highly shameful in most Muslim communities), she was shot dead by the gunman who came with her mother to their meeting. Imran's family members were never prosecuted for her murder. Widney Brown, an advocate for the U.S.-based nonprofit group Human Rights Watch, says that the murders of women to protect family honor over offenses such as divorce or adultery are common in Muslim societies: "In many cases women are buried in unmarked graves and all records of their existence are wiped out."

Islam Is a Peaceful Religion

Some people, however, vehemently refute the idea that Islam promotes violence. They say the very name of the religion means "peace" in Arabic, and that Islam has a long history of tolerance of other faiths. As evidence, they point to the tens of millions of Christians who have lived peacefully in Muslim countries for almost fourteen hundred years since the religion was founded in the seventh century. Some prominent Muslim women assert that Islam promotes not only tolerance for other faiths but also equality and democracy; they contend that the religion opposes repression, force, and violence toward women.

Among the leading spokeswomen for the religion is former Pakistan prime minister Benazir Bhutto. Bhutto identifies three

Islamic traditions that are in accordance with the liberal democratic spirit of the West. "Islam is committed to tolerance and
equality, and it is committed by Koranic definition to the principles of democracy," says Bhutto. "Three key principles in Islam
point to democracy: consultation, known as *shura;* consensus,
known as *ijmaa;* and independent judgment, known as *itjihad.*"

Echoing Bhutto's sentiments about Islam's commitment to
democracy and equality, Sharifa Alkhateeb of the Washington,
D.C.–based North American Council for Muslim Women, says
that the Koran details a long list of women's rights—to own
property, engage in business, choose a marriage partner, divorce,
claim inheritance, receive an education, and be treated with respect and dignity. She says that Islamic practices are often misunderstood in the West, particularly Muslim women's attire:

> There is such a horrible negative image associated
> with the [head] scarf: of ignorance, dirty hair or
> terrorism. . . . Muslim American women have been
> denied jobs by airlines, restaurants, even universi-
> ties because of their attire. . . . The main reason we
> wear a head covering is to set ourselves apart from
> males and insist they observe us as human beings,
> with ideas and concepts, rather than be distracted
> by hair and perfume and makeup.

Prominent people who defend Islam are not confined to
the Muslim community. Prince Charles, heir to the British
throne, has said publicly several times that Western civilization
has much to learn from Islam. Others have praised Islam for
uniting people across national, ethnic, and racial boundaries,
saying the religion can potentially restore peace and harmony
to humankind. Lady Evelyn Zeinab, an eminent British convert
to Islam, writes about her decision to become a Muslim: "The
more I read and studied [about Islam], the more convinced I
became that [it] is the one religion most conducive to bring humanity peace and happiness . . . and to solve the world's per-
plexing problems."

The Consequences of Beliefs About Islam

The debate over whether Islam is the cause of or solution to the
world's problems and conflicts continues. Ultimately, the conclusion may depend on whether the observer chooses to focus
on the acts of a small but vicious group of Islamic extremists or

the lives of hundreds of millions of peaceful Muslims through-out the world. There are, however, important consequences of the way people think about the world's fastest-growing religion. As seasoned British diplomat to Middle Eastern countries Patrick Bannerman says, "How non-Muslims think of Islam conditions the manner in which they deal with Muslims, which in turn conditions how Muslims think of and deal with non-Muslims."

The fate of humanity in the twenty-first century may well be determined by whether Muslims and non-Muslims choose violence, retribution, and fear or tolerance, cooperation, and compassion in their dealings with each other. It is a choice all Muslim and non-Muslim world citizens make when they en-counter one another; it is a choice of the utmost consequence. In her speech in Washington, D.C., to a large gathering of Mus-lims and non-Muslims after the tragedy of September 11, 2001, Benazir Bhutto concluded, "Ladies and gentlemen, . . . [war] be-tween the West and the Islamic world is far from inevitable, un-less we make it so."

1

Islam Declares Holy War on America and Its Allies

Osama bin Laden

Osama bin Laden, born in 1957 in Saudi Arabia, is head of the Islamic terrorist organization al Qaeda. According to Western intelligence agencies, Bin Laden masterminded the September 11, 2001, attack on the United States and continues to direct terrorist assaults on civilians throughout the Western world. The following declaration of jihad, or holy war, against America, made in 1998, was part of the evidence cited by Western authorities that linked Bin Laden to the 2001 attack.

At this unfortunate time in Muslim history the Arabian Peninsula is being attacked by many nations, but most particularly by the United States of America. For more than seven years America has occupied Arab lands and humiliated the Muslim people. The Americans continue to support the Jewish occupation of the Muslim holy city of Jerusalem, and now they are looting and plundering Iraq. Throughout Muslim history Allah has commanded his followers to repulse the enemy who destroys Muslim lands. In accordance with Allah's orders all Muslims must kill Americans, both civilians and military, wherever they may be found. Allah will reward in heaven all those who sacrifice their lives for his glory.

Praise be to Allah who revealed the Book [the Koran, the Muslim holy book], controls the clouds, defeats factional-

Osama bin Laden, "Jihad Against Jews and Crusaders: World Islamic Front Statement," http://fas.usda.gov, February 23, 1998.

ism, and says in His Book: "But when the forbidden months are past, then fight and slay the pagans wherever ye find them, seize them, beleaguer them, and lie in wait for them in every stratagem (of war)"; and peace be upon our Prophet, Muham- mad Bin-'Abdallah, who said: "I have been sent with the sword between my hands to ensure that no one but Allah is wor- shipped, Allah who put my livelihood under the shadow of my spear and who inflicts humiliation and scorn on those who dis- obey my orders."

> *" Nations are attacking Muslims like people fighting over a plate of food. "*

The Arabian Peninsula has never—since Allah made it flat, created its desert, and encircled it with seas—been stormed by any forces like the crusader armies spreading in it like locusts, eating its riches and wiping out its plantations. All this is hap- pening at a time in which nations are attacking Muslims like people fighting over a plate of food. In the light of the grave sit- uation and the lack of support, we and you are obliged to dis- cuss current events, and we should all agree on how to settle the matter.

American Occupation of Arab Lands

No one argues today about three facts that are known to every- one; we will list them, in order to remind everyone:

> First, for over seven years the United States has been occupying the lands of Islam in the holiest of places, the Arabian Peninsula, plundering its riches, dictating to its rulers, humiliating its people, terror- izing its neighbors, and turning its bases in the Peninsula into a spearhead through which to fight the neighboring Muslim peoples.
>
> If some people have in the past argued about the fact of the occupation, all the people of the Penin- sula have now acknowledged it. The best proof of this is the Americans' continuing aggression against the Iraqi people using the Peninsula as a staging

post, even though all its rulers are against their territories being used to that end, but they are helpless.

Second, despite the great devastation inflicted on the Iraqi people by the crusader-Zionist alliance, and despite the huge number of those killed, which has exceeded 1 million . . . despite all this, the Americans are once again trying to repeat the horrific massacres, as though they are not content with the protracted blockade imposed after the ferocious war or the fragmentation and devastation.

So here they come to annihilate what is left of this people and to humiliate their Muslim neighbors.

Third, if the Americans' aims behind these wars are religious and economic, the aim is also to serve the Jews' petty state and divert attention from its occupation of Jerusalem and murder of Muslims there. The best proof of this is their eagerness to destroy Iraq, the strongest neighboring Arab state, and their endeavor to fragment all the states of the region such as Iraq, Saudi Arabia, Egypt, and Sudan into paper statelets and through their disunion and weakness to guarantee Israel's survival and the continuation of the brutal crusade occupation of the Peninsula.

> *We . . . call on every Muslim who believes in Allah and wishes to be rewarded to comply with Allah's order to kill the Americans.*

All these crimes and sins committed by the Americans are a clear declaration of war on Allah, his messenger, and Muslims. And ulema [Islamic scholars] have throughout Islamic history unanimously agreed that the jihad is an individual duty if the enemy destroys the Muslim countries. This was revealed by [classical Islamic scholars] Imam Bin-Qadamah in "Al-Mughni," Imam al-Kisa'i in "Al-Bada'i," al-Qurtubi in his interpretation, and the shaykh of al-Islam in his books, where he said: "As for the fighting to repulse [an enemy], it is aimed at defending sanctity and religion, and it is a duty as agreed [by the ulema]. Nothing is more sacred than belief except repulsing an enemy who is attacking religion and life."

Muslims Must Kill Americans and Their Allies

On that basis, and in compliance with Allah's order, we issue the following fatwa[1] to all Muslims:

The ruling to kill the Americans and their allies—civilians and military—is an individual duty for every Muslim who can do it in any country in which it is possible to do it, in order to liberate the al-Aqsa Mosque [Muslim noble sanctuary in Jerusalem] and the holy mosque [Mecca] from their grip, and in order for their armies to move out of all the lands of Islam, defeated and unable to threaten any Muslim. This is in accordance with the words of Almighty Allah, "and fight the pagans all together as they fight you all together," and "fight them until there is no more tumult or oppression, and there prevail justice and faith in Allah."

This is in addition to the words of Almighty Allah: "And why should ye not fight in the cause of Allah and of those who, being weak, are ill-treated (and oppressed)?—women and children, whose cry is: 'Our Lord, rescue us from this town, whose people are oppressors; and raise for us from thee one who will help!'"

We—with Allah's help—call on every Muslim who believes in Allah and wishes to be rewarded [in heaven] to comply with Allah's order to kill the Americans and plunder their money wherever and whenever they find it. We also call on Muslim ulema, leaders, youths, and soldiers to launch the raid on Satan's[2] U.S. troops and the devil's supporters allying with them, and to displace those who are behind them so that they may learn a lesson.

Almighty Allah said: "O ye who believe, give your response to Allah and His Apostle, when He calleth you to that which will give you life. And know that Allah cometh between a man and his heart, and that it is He to whom ye shall all be gathered."

Almighty Allah also says: "O ye who believe, what is the

1. A fatwa is an interpretation of a verse in the Koran or other Muslim text, usually by a Muslim scholar. American scholar of Islam Bernard Lewis points out that Bin Laden's use of the term *fatwa* as "decree" is an inappropriate use of the term according to the doctrine of Islam.   2. Ayatollah Khomeini of Iran first called America the "great Satan" in the 1980s.

matter with you, that when ye are asked to go forth in the cause of Allah, ye cling so heavily to the earth! Do ye prefer the life of this world to the hereafter? But little is the comfort of this life, as compared with the hereafter. Unless ye go forth, He will punish you with a grievous penalty, and put others in your place; but Him ye would not harm in the least. For Allah hath power over all things."

Almighty Allah also says: "So lose no heart, nor fall into despair. For ye must gain mastery if ye are true in faith."

2

Many Islamic Leaders Advocate Peaceful Relations with the West

John L. Esposito

John L. Esposito, one of America's leading scholars on Islam, is a professor of religion and international affairs and the director for the Center for Muslim Understanding at Georgetown University in Washington, D.C. He is author of The Islamic Threat: Myth or Reality? *(1999) and* What Everyone Needs to Know About Islam *(2002).*

A number of prominent commentators say that Islamic violence against the West is the result of an inevitable clash of incompatible civilizations. These commentators fail to acknowledge the diversity among the world's Muslim countries and the millions of practicing Muslims who live in the West and enjoy Western economic opportunities and political freedoms. As militant Islamic leaders continue to dominate news headlines, the Western public learns little about the influential Muslim leaders who call for dialogue and cooperation with the West. Malaysia's opposition spokesman Anwar Ibrahim, Iran's president Mohammad Khatami, and Indonesia's former president Abdurrahman Wahid, for example, advocate very different Islamic perspectives from those of the terrorist Osama bin Laden. Although these leaders are faithful adherents of Islam, they say that mutually beneficial exchanges between Islam and the West are possible and desirable. Policy makers in the twenty-first century must resist seeing the world in terms of polarized opposites and identify new forms of government that respect the importance of religion in many of the world's nations. Defining Islam as a monolithic entity is no longer plausible as the boundaries between the Western world and the Islamic world evaporate.

In a controversial 1993 article, "The Clash of Civilizations?," [American scholar] Samuel P. Huntington warned that a "clash of civilizations [between Islam and the West] will dominate global politics" and precipitated a heated worldwide debate among scholars, political leaders, commentators, and the media. Many in the Muslim world saw this important American academic and opinion maker, who had also held a prominent position in government, as articulating what they always thought was the West's attitude toward Islam. If some academics and government officials were quick to distance themselves from Huntington's position, the sales of his subsequent book, its translation into many languages, and the sheer number of international conferences and publications that addressed the question demonstrated that there was "a market for clash." The attacks [on the United States by Islamic terrorists] of September 11 [2001] and the global threat of [Islamic terrorist leader] Osama bin Laden and [his terrorist group] al-Qaeda have resurrected a knee-jerk response of "the clash of civilizations" for an easy answer to the question, Why do they hate us?

Complex Causes of Terrorism

Huntington, like many others today, played into old stereotypes by characterizing Islam and the West as age-old enemies—"Conflict along the fault line between Western and Islamic civilizations has been going on for 1300 years"—and by citing Islam's resistance to secular Western models as necessarily hostile to human rights and progress—"Western ideas of individualism, liberalism, constitutionalism, human rights, equality, liberty, the rule of law, democracy, free markets, the separation of church and state, often have little resonance in Islamic [and other] . . . cultures."

In his 1997 follow-up book, Huntington concluded that "Islam's borders are bloody and so are its innards." His blanket condemnation went beyond Islamic fundamentalism to Islam itself: "The underlying problem for the West is not Islamic fundamentalism. It is Islam, a different civilization whose people are convinced of the superiority of their culture, and are obsessed with the inferiority of their power." Though Huntington has now significantly refined his position, September 11 unleashed new, updated versions as many found it more expedient to fall back on convenient stereotypes of a monolithic Islam and historic clash of civilizations rather than to examine the complex causes of terrorism.

> **//** *Many found it . . . expedient to fall back on . . . stereotypes of a . . . historic clash of civilizations rather than to examine the complex causes of terrorism.* **//**

Ironically, the clash of cultures appears as evident with reference to our allies in the Muslim world as with our enemies. Whatever the common economic and political interests, primarily centered on oil, the contrasts between Saudi Arabia and the United States are stark. The religious and cultural traditions of America's long-time ally—religiously puritanical and exclusivist worldview, sexually segregated society, lack of political parties and elections, punishment of theft by amputation, prohibition of building churches or practicing Christianity—as well as the fact that bin Laden and so many of the hijackers of September 11 were Saudi, indicate that we live in two different worlds. Similarly, the declared war of religious extremists and terrorists against entrenched Muslim governments and the West—all in the name of Islam—seems to underscore the incompatibility of Islam and democracy. However, while the actions of extremist groups and of authoritarian governments, religious and nonreligious, reinforce this perception of a cultural clash, the facts on the ground present a more complex picture.

Muslim Diversity

Neither the Muslim world nor the West is monolithic. Common sources of identity (language, faith, history, culture) yield when national or regional interests are at stake. While some Muslims have achieved a transient unity in the face of a common enemy, as in the Iranian Revolution, their solidarity quickly dissipates once danger subsides and competing interests again prevail. The evidence that there is no monolithic Islam is abundant. The inability of Arab nationalism/socialism, Saudi Arabia's pan-Islam, or Iran's Islamic Republic revolution to unite and mobilize the Arab and Muslim worlds, the competition and conflict between countries like Egypt, Libya, Sudan, and Saudi Arabia, the disintegration of the Arab (Iraq and the Gulf states) coalition against Iran after the Iran-Iraq war, and the subsequent Iraqi invasion of Kuwait and divisions in the Muslim world evident in the 1991 Gulf war are but a few examples. As James Piscatori observed, "The problem with assuming a unified response is that it conceals the reality of . . . entrenched national differences and national interests among Muslims." The failure of Osama bin Laden, like [Iraq's former dictator] Saddam Hussein and [Iran's former leader Ayatollah] Khomeini before him, to effectively mobilize the Islamic world in his unholy war, despite his global terrorist network, is a reminder that Muslims, like every global religious community, are indeed diverse. Moreover, as Islamic history makes abundantly clear, mainstream Islam, in law and theology as well as in practice, in the end has always rejected or marginalized extremists and terrorists from the Kharijites [seventh-century Islamic extremists] and Assassins [twelfth-century Islamic extremists] to contemporary radical movements such as al-Qaeda.

Islam and Capitalism Are Compatible

In responding to the attacks of September 11, some charged that the clash of civilizations revolved around conflict with our modern Western way of life, with, for example, democracy, women's rights, and capitalism. In fact, capitalism exists in the Muslim world both in home-grown forms as well as Western-inspired versions. The issue for many in the Muslim world is not capitalism but the dangers of Western economic hegemony and its side effects. In fact, Islam does not have any problem with many of the essentials of Western capitalism. It is important to recall that Muhammad's early followers included prosperous merchants. He himself engaged in financial and commercial transactions to make a living. The Quran, *hadith* (traditions about what the Prophet said and did), and Muslim historical experience affirm the right to private property and trade and commerce. As Maxime Rodinson, a French scholar and Marxist, wrote in his *Islam and Capitalism:* "Economic activity, the search for profit, trade, and consequently, production for the market, are looked upon with no less favor by Muslim tradition than by the Koran itself." Mosques throughout the world, such as the Umayyad mosque in Damascus and the magnificent mosques of old Cairo and Teheran, are often adjoined by magnificent bazaars. Traders and businessmen were among the most successful sectors in society and were responsible for the spread of their faith.

> *The evidence that there is no monolithic Islam is abundant.*

Perhaps the best response to those who ask whether Islam and capitalism are compatible is to look at the lives of the millions of Muslims who live and work in our midst in America and Europe. Many have come here to enjoy freedom and the opportunities offered by our economic and political systems. Like other religious and ethnic minorities before them, they too struggle with issues of identity and assimilation but not with their desire to enjoy the best that we represent. . . .

Voices of Islamic Reform

Because acts of violence and terrorism grab the headlines, we seem to know a lot more about Islamic advocates of a "clash," the militant jihadists [Islamic holy warriors], than about those who are working toward a peaceful revolution and civilizational dialogue. Today, Islam's encounter with the West and the need for Islamic reform are being addressed by intellectuals, religious leaders, and activists alike. Like the Islamic modernist movements in the late nineteenth and early twentieth centuries and later the Islamic (fundamentalist) movements of the Muslim Brotherhood [Egyptian Islamic extremist group] and the Jamaat-i-Islami [Pakistan's religious party], today's Islamically oriented intellectuals and activists continue the process of Islamic modernization and reform. However, today's reformers represent a creative new stage in that they not only reformulate Islam conceptually but also implement their ideas through their positions in government and the public arena.

Three remarkable examples reflect the diverse voices of Islamic reform and civilizational dialogue that can be heard from the Middle East to Asia. Active as intellectuals and politicians, Anwar Ibrahim, former deputy prime minister of Malaysia, Mohammad Khatami, president of the Islamic Republic of Iran, and Abdurrahman Wahid, former president of Indonesia, have played important roles in defining the terms for an intercivilizational dialogue, rather than a clash of civilizations. At the same time, each takes a position that is uniquely different from the West's, reflective of his own culture and political environment. Though all three object to concepts of development that presume the desirability of Western secularization for Muslim societies, they recognize the strengths and weaknesses of Western-style modernity. Thus, they advocate an active two-way-dialogue among civilizations, especially between Islam and the West.

Malaysia's Anwar Ibrahim

When Anwar Ibrahim, sometimes called "Malaysia's own Islamic zealot," joined the government of Prime Minister Mahathir Mohammed in 1980, he stunned friends and foes alike. Nevertheless, he showed that he could succeed in both worlds, rapidly evolving from a charismatic opposition leader to deputy prime minister and finance minister. Ibrahim worked effectively with diverse political forces and navigated Malaysia's complex multireligious (Muslim, Christian, Hindu, Buddhist) and multiethnic (Malay, Chinese, Indian) society. He had impressed many at home and abroad with his ability to bridge religions and cultures and to work effectively to achieve common goals. He had earned the reputation of "an unabashed globalist well suited to the modern world of markets and media" and a "liberal" [according to an editorial in the *Wall Street Journal* on October 30, 1998]. Eighteen years later, he would be tried and convicted on politically inspired charges, an action condemned internationally by many political and religious leaders and human rights organizations. He remains, although in prison,[1] a significant voice on issues of sociopolitical and economic development, advocating pluralism in multireligious societies and intercivilizational dialogue as the only alternative to a deadly clash of civilizations.

A pragmatic man of politics as well as of faith, Ibrahim argued that both Marxist and Western models of secular materi-

---

1. Ibrahim was released from prison on September 3, 2004, after six years in confinement.

alism had failed. "Marxism . . . severs man from his moorings in faith. . . . There was no place for ethics, morality or spirituality," and the West also rejects "any reference to moral and ethical considerations. Cultural preservation is regarded as retrogressive in the march for development."

> *The issue for many in the Muslim world is not capitalism but the dangers of Western economic hegemony and its side effects.*

In contrast to more conservative Islamist groups that called for a return to Islamic law, Ibrahim said,

> [Southeast Asian Muslims] would rather strive to improve the welfare of the women and children in their midst than spend their days elaborately defining the nature and institutions of the ideal Islamic state. They do not believe it makes one less a Muslim to promote economic growth, to master the information revolution and to demand justice for women.

Living in Harmony

Anwar Ibrahim's Islam is a dynamic, developing tradition that responds to diverse times and places. He rejected the conservative imitation (*taqlid*) of the past in favor of independent analysis and reinterpretation (*ijtihad*), believing that Islam is "a pragmatic religion whose real strength and dynamism was in its ongoing revitalization. . . ." A strong proponent of East-West dialogue, he believes Islam is also inclusive, and as in the past, so too today Islam should be open to all cultures.

Pluralism and tolerance based upon mutual respect and understanding are cornerstones of Anwar Ibrahim's vision of a civilizational dialogue or *convivencia*, that has deep roots in medieval Islamic history. *Convivencia* (living together) alludes to the spirit of Roger II's twelfth-century Sicily and Muslim rule in the Iberian Peninsula in centers like Toledo, Cordoba, and Granada. In Iberia, Christians, Muslims, and Jews lived together in a context of social intercourse and cultural exchange. It was a time of prosperity and achievement; the arts, literature, poetry, astronomy, and medicine flourished. Many Christians became known as Mozarabs because of the extent to which they adopted elements of Arab dress, culture, and language, including Arabic names. Some Christian scholars wrote in Arabic instead of Latin.

Ibrahim finds the roots of *convivencia* supported both in Islamic history and in the Quran, as illustrated by the verse, "Oh mankind! Verily we have created you all from a male and a female, and have made you into nations and tribes that you may come to know one another."

> *We seem to know a lot more about Islamic advocates of a 'clash' . . . than about those who are working toward a peaceful revolution.*

Convivencia, for Ibrahim, is an Islamic form of pluralism, a vision quite different from the typical Islamist programs that make a place for non-Muslims in a traditionally conceived Islamic society. It is based on the primacy of social and economic justice and equality, recognized as fundamental to other religions as well as Islam. This pluralist vision is the foundation for his call for civilizational dialogue:

> For us, the divine imperative as expressed in the Qur'an is unambiguous. Humanity has been created to form tribes, races and nations, whose differences in physical characteristics, languages and modes of thought are but the means for the purpose of *lita'arafu*—"getting to know one another."

Ibrahim appreciated the urgency of diffusing global confrontations, stressing that *convivencia* is a necessity for progress. However, it must be an encounter among equals. Old Western imperialist attitudes of their "civilizing mission" as well as fundamentalist rejections of the enemy West threaten human survival.

Iran's Mohammad Khatami

For more than twenty years America and Iran were locked in a cycle of "mutual satanization." Memories of the Iranian revolution, American diplomats held hostage, Iran's ambitious attempts to export its revolution, and Ayatollah Khomeini's *fatwa* [religious ruling] condemning to death British author Salman Rushdie for his book *The Satanic Verses* made Iran the epitome of an Islamic global threat.

> *In our world, dialogue among civilizations is an absolute imperative.*

In August 1997, eighteen years after the Iranian revolution had stunned the world, the newly elected president of the Islamic Republic surprised the international community in his inaugural address. Mohammad Khatami called for a dialogue of civilizations, "in our world, dialogue among civilizations is an absolute imperative." The president of a country that America labeled terrorist became one of the major advocates for a new policy debate within Iran and within the global community about the clash of civilizations.

The new climate was dramatically conveyed to the world in a televised CNN interview with Christiane Amanpour [CNN's chief international correspondent] in which Khatami surprised many by stating that Western civilization and the United States were worthy of respect, citing in particular the experience of the Pilgrims at Plymouth as an important event in affirming religious freedom, and the importance of the example of Abraham Lincoln.

Mutually Beneficial Exchanges

Khatami articulated a distinctive alternative approach to relations between Islam and the West. The old-fashioned jihad–clash-of-civilizations perspective offered stark alternatives of victory or defeat. Khatami's vision combined a nonmilitant jihadist defense of Islamic identity and values with a call for civilizational dialogue by which all societies could benefit through the exchange of information and ideas.

Khatami's model for dialogue does not preclude strong criticism of Western policies, especially those of the United States. Speaking of a flawed U.S. policy of domination, Khatami denounced America's use of sanctions against Iran and others.

America, he said, attempts to "impose their own domestic law on the world . . . [but the] world will not tolerate a master any more—not only will we not tolerate a master, neither will the world." Thus, Khatami combines strong affirmation of Iran's principles and critique of U.S. policy with an emphatic advocacy of the dialogue of civilizations and of improved Iranian-U.S. relations in particular.

Mohammad Khatami's dialogue of civilizations is an alternative both to the old militant jihadist rhetoric and to uncritical dependence on the West (what some have termed "westoxication"). In contrast to the hard-line position of [Iran's clerical leader] Ayatollah Ali Khamenei, Khomeini's successor as Supreme Guide of the Islamic republic, Khatami boldly asserts that Islamic reform, open to a dynamic interaction with Western civilization, must build a bridge between tradition and modernity:

> We must concede that the incompatibility of modern civilization with our tradition-bound civilization is one of the most important causes of the crisis in our society. What is to be done? Should we insist on remaining immersed in our tradition, or should we melt fully into Western civilization? Or is there another way of removing this contradiction?

Khatami's vision of the history and development of civilizations is dynamic; civilizations constantly change and evolve. The West is the latest,

> but not the ultimate human civilization, which like all other human artifacts, is tentative and susceptible to decay. . . . Civilizations change and there is no such thing as an ultimate and eternal civilization.

Strategy to Strengthen Islam

Khatami believes that at the beginning of the twenty-first century the need is for the creation of a new civilization. However, his call for dialogue must be seen within the context of his particular worldview, which differs from that of many in America and Europe. Many in the West assume that dialogue with the West means that eventually non-Western peoples will see the advantages of Western civilization and become more Western-ized. This would be a complete misunderstanding of Khatami's vision of dialogue, which is not a passive policy of accommodation but a competitive strategy for strengthening and transforming Islamic civilization. It transcends a militant vision of jihad and offers a way to avoid destructive conflict. Dialogue with the West is an important way of strengthening Islam. Khatami's vision holds out the hope that, as the West evolves and possibly declines, Islam will regain its position as the leading progressive world civilization.

> *Khatami's vision of dialogue . . . is not a passive policy of accommodation but a competitive strategy for strengthening . . . Islamic civilization.*

In the continued encounter of Islam and the West in the twenty-first century, Khatami's dialogue of civilizations reflects a significant perspective very different from that of both Western analysts such as Samuel Huntington and old-style Islamic advocates of militant jihad such as [twentieth-century Egyptian Islamic fundamentalist] Sayyid Qutb and, more recently, Osama bin Laden.

Indonesia's Abdurrahman Wahid

In October 1999, Abdurrahman Wahid, leader of the Nahdatul Ulama (Renaissance of Religious Scholars), the biggest (35 million members) Islamic organization in the world's largest Muslim country, became the first elected president in Indonesia's history. Nahdatul Ulama (NU) is a predominantly conservative, rural-based sociocultural organization founded in 1926 to defend the interests of traditional Islam and counter the threat of modernism. Wahid, however, is best described as a modern, urban, liberal Muslim intellectual. As a religious leader and social and political reformer, he has staunchly opposed those who would reassert Islam's role in politics and has warned of the dangers of Islamic fundamentalism.

Bridging the worlds of traditional Islam and modern thought, Wahid espouses a reformist intellectual synthesis and social agenda that distinguishes between unchanging religious doctrines or laws and those that can be altered to accommodate social change. Wahid is among a generation of reformers who advocate a progressive Islam, one that is inclusive, democratic, pluralistic, and tolerant. Wahid advocates a cosmopolitan Islam, the product of creative reinterpretation or reformulation, responsive to the demands of modern life and reflecting Indonesian Islam's diverse religious and ethnic history and communities. . . .

A political realist who recognized the needs to create national unity in the face of communalism, to establish the rule of law, and to develop viable economic frameworks for the equitable distribution of wealth, Wahid also put his finger on a major cause of violence and terrorism in Muslim countries. Most governments in the Muslim world rely on sociopolitical engineering, authoritarianism, political suppression, and violence to impose their vision. Wahid maintains that governments close their eyes to a fundamental issue of development when they reduce national problems solely to political and socioeconomic and technical factors. The failure to address the relationship of faith to national identity and to institution building contributes to instability and risks "massive social explosions." Governments that rely on social control rather than consultation, that employ violence and repression, create a climate that contributes to radicalization and violence against the state. Wahid has astutely identified the heart of the struggle in Islam today. Movements are faced with two options, "the choice of following either a radical approach or a gradual response in their struggle for social justice, equal treatment before the law and freedom of expression."

Islam Is Not Monolithic

Anwar Ibrahim, Mohammad Khatami, and Abdurrahman Wahid are but three of many voices for Islamic reform. They demonstrate that there is no essentialist or monolithic Islam or Muslim society. All may share a common faith, at times articulate an Islamically inspired worldview, and use Islam as a source of legitimacy and mobilization. Still, their visions, goals, and strategies are shaped as much by diverse political and cultural contexts as by faith. They challenge those who see the world of the early twenty-first century in polarities, either confrontation and conflict or dialogue and cooperation, to appreciate the limitations and failures of old paradigms and to develop new paradigms for governance and policy that are sensitive to the importance of religion and culture.

Finally, in an increasingly global society, defining Islam and the Muslim world monolithically becomes more difficult as clear boundaries between Islam and the West evaporate. Not only are Muslim countries, societies, and institutions deeply involved with non-Muslim societies and communities but, more important, Islam is so present in America and Europe that Muslims have become part of the fabric of Western societies, as citizens, professionals, and neighbors. Many Muslims are third- and fourth-generation citizens in Western societies, no more and no less American or European than Jews, Christians, and Hindus.

3

Islam Is a
Religion of Peace

George W. Bush

George W. Bush is the forty-third president of the United States.

The Muslim terrorists who attacked the United States on September 11, 2001, violated the tenets of the Islamic faith. These terrorists do not represent the true Islam, which is a religion of peace that gives comfort to millions of Americans. American Muslims are appalled at the tragedy, for they love America as much as other Americans do.

The American people were appalled and outraged at last Tuesday's attacks [on September 11, 2001, when Islamic terrorists attacked the World Trade Center and other American targets]. And so were Muslims all across the world. Both Americans and Muslim friends and citizens, tax-paying citizens, and Muslims in nations were just appalled and could not believe what we saw on our TV screens.

These acts of violence against innocents violate the fundamental tenets of the Islamic faith. And it's important for my fellow Americans to understand that.

The English translation is not as eloquent as the original Arabic, but let me quote from the Koran itself: In the long run, evil in the extreme will be the end of those who do evil. For that they rejected the signs of Allah and held them up to ridicule.

The face of terror is not the true faith of Islam. That's not what Islam is all about. Islam is peace. These terrorists don't

George W. Bush, address at the Islamic Center of Washington, Washington, DC, September 17, 2001.

represent peace. They represent evil and war.

When we think of Islam we think of a faith that brings comfort to a billion people around the world. Billions of people find comfort and solace and peace. And that's made brothers and sisters out of every race—out of every race.

America counts millions of Muslims amongst our citizens, and Muslims make an incredibly valuable contribution to our country. Muslims are doctors, lawyers, law professors, members of the military, entrepreneurs, shopkeepers, moms and dads. And they need to be treated with respect. In our anger and emotion, our fellow Americans must treat each other with respect.

Women who cover their heads in this country must feel comfortable going outside their homes. Moms who wear cover must be not intimidated in America. That's not the America I know. That's not the America I value.

> *The face of terror is not the true face of Islam. That's not what Islam is all about. Islam is peace.*

I've been told that some fear to leave; some don't want to go shopping for their families; some don't want to go about their ordinary daily routines because, by wearing cover, they're afraid they'll be intimidated. That should not and that will not stand in America.

Those who feel like they can intimidate our fellow citizens to take out their anger don't represent the best of America, they represent the worst of humankind, and they should be ashamed of that kind of behavior.

This is a great country. It's a great country because we share the same values of respect and dignity and human worth. And it is my honor to be meeting with leaders who feel just the same way I do. They're outraged, they're sad. They love America just as much as I do. . . .

May God bless us all.

4

Islam Is Not a Peaceful Religion

Pat Robertson

Pat Robertson is a well-known American Christian evangelist, author, public speaker, and philanthropist. He founded the first Christian television network in the United States, the Christian Broadcasting Network (CBN), and a number of philanthropic organizations that operate in the Middle East and in other countries. He has written more than fourteen books, including Six Steps to Spiritual Revival, The Secret Kingdom, *and* The Ten Offenses.

Although many Muslims are peaceful, Islam is not a religion of peace. In the seventh century the religion's founder, the prophet Muhammad, was a warrior who preached holy war against all Christians and Jews. For the next several centuries Muslims established great empires in their desire to convert the world to their faith. Today an estimated 300 million Muslims consider America and much of the Western world the "land of war" and support the violence of Islamic suicide bombers against Western targets. The Western world and the Islamic world are fighting a war of ideology. Americans must understand Islamic history to know how to respond to the threat posed by this violent religion.

N ow it's been said of the Islamic faith that it is a peaceful religion. Obviously, there are millions of people in adherence to Islam who are very peaceful. They are lovely people. I have known many in dealing in the Middle East and you know many in America. So I would never begin to indict an entire religion.

Pat Robertson, "The Roots of Terrorism and a Strategy for Victory," address to the Economic Club of Detroit, March 25, 2002, www.patrobertson.com. Copyright © 2002 by The Christian Broadcasting Network, Inc. Reproduced by permission.

But I do think we need to step back in history because [American philosopher and poet] George Santayana said those who fail to learn the lessons of history are doomed to live them again.

Go back to the year 632 when Mohammed the progenitor and prophet of Islam died. Islam means submission—it doesn't mean peace. And he said the duty of his followers was to wage jihad against those who were not adherents to Islam. I have taken down some of the quotes in the Quran. And you'd be interested to know that in this holy book there are 120 references to warfare against the infidels. Mohammed himself was a warrior. He organized at least 50 raids in Saudi Arabia and personally was involved in warfare in 27 of them.

Mohammed's Sayings

And these are just some of the quotes from the one who founded this particular religion.

He said in the Hadith [record of the sayings of Mohammed]:

> The best deed of man is to believe in Allah and his Apostle. The second best deed is to participate in jihad in Allah's cause.

He also said in the [Muslim holy book the] Quran:

> Fight and slay the pagans wherever you find them. Seize them, beleaguer them and lie in wait for them. Fight them. Allah will punish them by your hands and bring them to disgrace.

He also said in the Quran:

> Oh ye that believe, take not Christians and Jews as your friends and protectors. Fight with them until there is no more persecution. Religion should only be for Allah.

And he also said:

> The last hour will not come until the Muslims fight the Jews and the Muslims kill them.

And you say, "Well this was very extreme," but I have before me a report from Fox news that is quoting the *Washington Post*. And this says, "Can it be true that Islamic schools in the U.S. teach hatred toward Americans, Christians and Jews. The *Washington Post* on Monday revealed that one such school outside

Washington D.C. uses textbooks teaching 11th graders that, 'The day of judgment can't come until Jesus Christ returns to earth, breaks the cross and converts everyone to Islam and until Muslims start attacking Jews.' At the same school they are taught that Osama bin Laden is 'simply the victim of prejudice against Muslims in America.' And the Washington Islamic Academy that teaches about 1,300 children and is founded by Saudi Arabia has a textbook that says 'One sign of the day of judgment will be that Muslims will fight and kill Jews who will hide behind trees and say 'Oh Muslim, oh servant of God there is a Jew hiding behind me. Come here and kill him.'"

Islamic History of Aggressive Wars

Now Ladies and Gentlemen, that is not a peaceful religion. And it's not something from ancient history. It's something from now. But if you go back in 632 with the death of Mohammed, he urged his followers to begin a jihad against all those who were not part of the Islamic tradition. He first of all took all of Saudi Arabia and waged war against it until they converted to Islam. He then moved across the formerly Christian populations of North Africa, and Islam spread as far as northern India to the east and all the way up into Spain. They then moved from Spain into southern France in the area of Bordeaux. And in 732 in something called the Battle of Tours a man named Charles Martel [eighth-century French king] organized the French Knights and they stood against the Muslim invaders and repulsed them. They went back into Spain where they had domination over Spain for about 760 years.

> *Mohammed himself was a warrior. He organized at least 50 raids in Saudi Arabia.*

And finally in 1492, the last of this influence was removed from Spain and there was a victory. But shortly thereafter on the other side of Islam came the Ottoman Empire which in 1492 overwhelmed the last Christian bastion in that Middle East area, the city of Constantinople, and installed their government and went from there up into the Balkans. In the battle of Kosovo they defeated the European Christians and began to brutalize the population until such time as they went all the way to the gates of Vienna in Austria where they were finally repulsed at the Battle of Vienna. And then in a great sea battle, they were finally overwhelmed. Otherwise, we all would have been speaking Arabic and the entire United States of America and Europe would have been given over to Islam. Now that is the history of so-called jihad. That is the war against the infidel that was preached by Mohammed and that is the history.

The Christians in the European areas had to fight for their lives lest they were forcibly converted to this religion.

Islam Is Not About Peace

In the Islamic teaching, once the Islamic people overcome a country, it is given to them by Allah. If someone takes it away from them, they are stealing from Allah. So guess what, there's a country in the Middle East called Israel and it is the belief of the entire Islamic world that this country is illegitimate that they have stolen Allah's territory. And it must be gotten back. I submit to you today that any peace negotiation that is being carried on right now is illusory. And whatever promises are being given by heads of state about peace will not last because in the mosques the people are being taught that Israel is illegitimate. [Palestine Liberation Organization leader] Yasar Arafat is the grandson of the Grand Mufti [Islamic spiritual leader] of Jerusalem. The Grand Mufti back in the days of World War II said, "Adolf Hitler only went part of the way. I want to finish what he began in regard to the Jews."

> *[Mohammed] first of all took all of Saudi Arabia and waged war against it until they converted to Islam.*

Now this is not peace. I believe those of us who love peace have to understand what we're up against. Again, I want to repeat, we're not looking at a huge group. There's a billion 200 million [1.2 billion] people who subscribe to Islam. Many of them don't understand these teachings. Many of them don't subscribe to them. Many of them have different points of view. I'm sure many of those adherents to Islam in the United States of America don't understand them. But in the radical Middle East these are the teachings that are being taught to millions of people. And if you estimate 250–300 million people subscribe to these extreme points of view, you have a very serious situation.

A Violent Clash of Civilizations

In the Islamic tradition everything that is taken by Islam is called the land of peace. Everything that is not taken is called Dar al-Harb. That means the land of war and you are sitting today in Dar al-Harb. Detroit Dar al-Harb. We are the land of war, and anyplace not under the land of peace is fair game for the land of war. This is why people will fly into buildings and kill themselves. This is why people will not have any compunction whatever to blow up innocent women and children. This is why extreme car bombers will go into a shopping center in Israel or a pizza parlor or a bar mitzvah and kill themselves in order to take thousands or hundreds of others out. Because they are told if they die in the cause of jihad, they will go immediately to paradise, and therefore they will be given 72 virgins as their reward.

We must understand what we are up against. We must understand the history.

I might add that in 1095 one of the popes said we have to fight fire with fire, and he authorized the Crusade. And he said those who participate in the Crusade against the Muslim will gain access to paradise in the event they are killed. So he launched on the side of Christianity a jihad comparable to what had been launched by the Muslims. And so when the president mentions a crusade, you can see everybody's back get up. Because these folks in the Middle East remember that. They remember. They remember history. They consider Spain as part of their territory. They consider Palestine as part of their territory. In the schools mentioned in the *Washington Post* article on the maps of the Middle East, there is no word for Israel. That whole section is called Palestine. Because that didn't belong to anybody except Allah. . . .

This is a religious struggle we are involved in. It is a clash of cultures. It is a clash of opposing points of view. It is a clash of different ideologies. And we need to understand what we're dealing with and how to deal with it.

5

Islam Promotes Terrorism

Ibn Warraq

Former Pakistani Muslim Ibn Warraq, who writes under a pseudonym, renounced his faith and became a secular humanist in early adulthood. In his published works, which include Why I Am Not a Muslim *(1995),* The Quest for Historical Muhammad *(2000), and* What the Koran Really Says: Language, Text, and Commentary *(2002), he critically examines the tenets of Islam.*

Apologists for Islam mislead the public when they say that the religion poses no real threat to global peace and stability. Islam motivated Osama bin Laden to instigate the terrorist attack on the United States on September 11, 2001, and the Koran instructs Muslims to wage war until the whole world is converted to Islam. Of all the world's religions, only Islam uses violent means to achieve its aims. It is not only the Islamic fundamentalists who pose a threat; it is the faith of Islam that jeopardizes human rights, individualism, democracy, and world peace.

To pretend that *Islam* has nothing to do with Terrorist Tuesday[1] is to wilfully ignore the obvious and to forever misinterpret events. Without Islam the long-term strategy and individual acts of violence by Usama bin Laden and his followers make little sense. The West needs to understand them in order to be able to deal with them and avoid past mistakes. We are

1. September 11, 2001, when Islamic terrorists attacked the United States

confronted with *Islamic* terrorists and must take seriously the *Islamic* component. Westerners in general, and Americans in particular, do not understand the passionate, religious, and anti-western convictions of Islamic terrorists. These God-intoxicated fanatics blindly throw away their lives in return for the Paradise of Seventy Two Virgins offered Muslim martyrs killed in the Holy War against all infidels.[2]

Jihad is "a religious war with those who are unbelievers in the mission of the Prophet Muhammad [the Prophet]. It is an incumbent religious duty, established in the Qur'an and in the Traditions as a divine institution, and enjoined specially for the purpose of advancing Islam and repelling evil from Muslims."

> *The totalitarian nature of Islam is nowhere more apparent than in the concept of* Jihad, *the Holy War, whose ultimate aim is to conquer the entire world.*

The world is divided into two spheres, *Dar al-Islam* [land of Islam or peace] and *Dar al-Harb* [land of war]. The latter, the Land of Warfare, is a country belonging to infidels which has not been subdued by Islam. The *Dar al-Harb* becomes the *Dar al-Islam*, the Land of Islam, upon the promulgation of the edicts of Islam. Thus the totalitarian nature of Islam is nowhere more apparent than in the concept of *Jihad*, the Holy War, whose ultimate aim is to conquer the entire world and submit it to the one true faith, to the law of Allah. To Islam alone has been granted the truth: there is no possibility of salvation outside it. Muslims must fight and kill in the name of Allah.

We read [in the Qur'an] (IX. 5–6): "Kill those who join other gods with God wherever you may find them";

IV.76: "Those who believe fight in the cause of God";

VIII.39–42: "Say to the Infidels: if they desist from their unbelief, what is now past shall be forgiven;

---

2. refers to the belief of some Islamic fundamentalists that if they die while fighting "infidels" they will receive the reward of seventy-two virgins and rivers of honey in Paradise

but if they return to it, they have already before them the doom of the ancients! Fight then against them till strife be at an end, and the religion be all of it God's."

Those who die fighting for the only true religion, Islam, will be amply rewarded in the life to come:

> IV.74: "Let those who fight in the cause of God who barter the life of this world for that which is to come; for whoever fights on God's path, whether he is killed or triumphs, We will give him a handsome reward."

What should we make with these further unfortunate verses from the Qur'an:
- Torment to Non-believers
- Only Islam [is] Acceptable. . .
- No friends with non-believers . . .
- Kill non-believers . . .
- Killing Idolators . . .
- Forcing non-believers to pay tax . . .
- Cast terror in the hearts, smite the neck and cut fingertips of unbelievers . . .
- Severe Punishment for atheists . . .
- Punishing for rejecting faith
- Non-believers go to hell
- Partial Believers go to hell too
- Sadistic punishments . . .

Islam Is at Fault

It is surely time for us who live in the West and enjoy freedom of expression to examine unflinchingly and unapologetically the tenets of these fanatics, including the Qur'an which divinely sanctions violence. We should unapologetically examine the life of the Prophet, who was not above political assassinations, and who was responsible for the massacre of the Jews.

"Ah, but you are confusing Islam with Islamic fundamentalism. The Real Islam has nothing to do with violence," apologists of Islam argue.

There may be moderate Muslims, but Islam itself is not moderate. There is no difference between Islam and Islamic fundamentalism: at most there is a difference of degree but not of kind.

All the tenets of Islamic fundamentalism are derived from the Qur'an, the *Sunna* [records of the life of Muhammad, the Muslim prophet], and the *Hadith* [records of the sayings and deeds of Muhammad]. Islamic fundamentalism is a totalitarian construct derived by Muslim jurists from the fundamental and defining texts of Islam. The fundamentalists, with greater logic and coherence than so-called moderate or liberal Muslims, have made Islam the basis of a radical utopian ideology that aims to replace capitalism and democracy as the reigning world system. Islamism accounts for the anti-American hatred to be found in places far from the Arab-Israeli conflict, like Nigeria and Afghanistan, demonstrating that the Middle East conflict cannot legitimately be used to explain this phenomenon called Islamism. A Palestinian involved in the WTC [World Trade Center] bombings would be seen as a martyr to the Palestinian cause, but even more as a martyr to Islam.

Islamic Fundamentalism Is More Violent

"Ah, but Islamic fundamentalism is like any other kind of fundamentalism, one must not demonise it. It is the result of political, social grievances. It must be explained in terms of economics and not religion," continue the apologists of Islam.

> *There may be moderate Muslims, but Islam itself is not moderate.*

There are enormous differences between Islamic fundamentalism and any other kind of modern fundamentalism. It is true that Hindu, Jewish, and Christian fundamentalists have been responsible for acts of violence, but these have been confined to particular countries and regions. Islamic fundamentalism has global aspirations: the submission of the entire world to the all-embracing *Shari'a*, Islamic Law, a fascist system of dictates designed to control every single act of all individuals. Nor do Hindus or Jews seek to convert the world to their religion. Christians do indulge in proselytism but no longer use acts of violence or international terrorism to achieve their aims.

Only Islam treats non-believers as inferior beings who are expendable in the drive to world hegemony. Islam justifies any means to achieve the end of establishing an Islamic world.

Islamic fundamentalists recruit among *Muslim* populations, they appeal to *Islamic* religious symbols, and they motivate their recruits with *Islamic* doctrine derived from the Qur'an. Economic poverty alone cannot explain the phenomenon of Islamism. Poverty in Brazil or Mexico has not resulted in Christian fundamentalist acts of international terror. Islamists are against what they see as Western materialism itself. Their choice is clear: Islam or *jahiliyya*. The latter term is redefined to mean modern-style *jahiliyya* of modern, democratic, industrialized societies of Europe and America, where man is under the dominion of man rather than Allah. They totally reject the values of the West, which they feel are poisoning Islamic culture. So, it is *not* just a question of economics, but of an entirely different worldview, which they wish to impose on the whole world. Sayyid Qutb, the very influential Egyptian Muslim thinker, said that

> dominion should be reverted to Allah alone, namely to Islam, that holistic system He conferred upon men. An all-out offensive, a jihad, should be waged against modernity so that this moral rearmament could take place. The ultimate objective is to re-establish the Kingdom of Allah upon earth. . . .

"The Islamic Threat" Is Not a Myth

Respect for other cultures, for other values than our own, is a hallmark of a civilised society. But multiculturalism is based on some fundamental misconceptions. First, there is the erroneous and sentimental belief that all cultures, deep down, have the same values; or, at least, if different, are equally worthy of respect. But the truth is that not all cultures have the same values, and not all values are worthy of respect. There is nothing sacrosanct about customs or cultural traditions: they can change under criticism. After all, the secularist values of the West are not much more than two hundred years old.

If these other values are destructive of our own cherished values, are we not justified in fighting them both by intellectual means, that is by reason and argument, and criticism, and by legal means, by making sure the laws and constitution of the country are respected by all? It becomes a duty to defend those values that we would live by. But here Western intellectuals have sadly failed in defending Western values, such as rationalism, social pluralism, human rights, the rule of law, representative government, individualism (in the sense that every individual counts, and no individual should be sacrificed for some utopian future collective end), freedom of expression, freedom of and from religion, the rights of minorities, and so on.

Instead, the so-called experts on Islam in Western universities, in the media, in the churches and even in government bureaus have become apologists for Islam. They bear some responsibility for creating an atmosphere little short of intellectual terrorism where any criticism of Islam is denounced as fascism, racism, or "orientalism."[3] They bear some responsibility for lulling the public into thinking that "The Islamic Threat" is a myth. It is our duty to fight this intellectual terrorism. It is our duty to defend the values of liberal democracy.

One hopes that the U.S. government will not now act in such a way that more innocent lives are lost, albeit on the other side of the globe. One hopes that even now there is a legal way out in international courts of law. The situation is far more delicate and complex than a simple battle between good and evil, the solution is not to beat hell out of all Arabs and Muslims but neither is it to pretend that Islam had nothing to do with it, for that would be to bury one's head in the Sands of Arab [desert regions of the Arabian peninsula].

3. depicts Arab culture as prototypical, antiwestern, and untrustworthy

6

Islam Has Been Hijacked by Terrorists

Reuven Firestone

Rabbi, author, and scholar Reuven Firestone is professor of medieval Judaism and Islam at Hebrew Union College in Los Angeles. He is author of numerous books on Islam and Judaism, including Jihad: The Origin of Holy War in Islam *(1999) and* Children of Abraham: An Introduction to Judaism for Muslims *(2001).*

Islam is a great and compassionate religion that has been misrepresented by so-called "Muslim scholars." Although the Koran does contain some violent incitations, it must be remembered that the Bible also contains such passages. With both texts, readers need to understand the context of the inflammatory lines rather than taking them as literal invocations to violence. Furthermore, one can just as easily find lines urging people to have compassion for the needy and the poor in the Koran. Islamic law is open to many interpretations and has been manipulated by repressive regimes to subjugate their people, and by terrorists to justify evil acts. Islam is not to blame for the murder of more than three thousand people on September 11, 2001. Rather, terrorists alone are responsible for these atrocious acts committed in the name of the great faith of Islam.

The queries have come in steadily since the great increase in suicide bombings by Muslim Palestinians during [2001] but since [the terrorist attacks on the United States on] Sept. 11,

[2001,] they have come virtually non-stop, "Does Islam condone suicide? Does Islam condone killing noncombatants? Does Islam teach that a martyr who enters heaven gets the pleasure of 70 virgins? Does Islam really teach the universal doctrine of 'Islam or the sword?' Does Islam hate Jews and Judaism?" or, "Does Islam fundamentally hate anyone and anything not Muslim or Islamic?"

> *[Jews] have [also] suffered the abuse of religious character assassination by those who not only have hated us, but also by those who have feared us.*

Americans know almost nothing about Islam beyond what they pick up from films and novels and news reports (much of it erroneous). Israelis probably know even less, though many have the bad habit of claiming (with some swagger) that they know Muslims because they live with them. The truth of the matter is that Israelis don't live with Muslims, hardly see them beyond what they see on their own televisions, and tend to have an extremely distorted view of Islam. We few who know something about Islam are bombarded with questions and asked for interviews, but given the hurry and the nature of media discourse, the short answers often confuse more than clarify.

Simplistic clarifications by so-called "Muslim scholars" often confuse the situation even more, because virtually any Muslim can claim to be a scholar and speak on behalf of Islam. From my own experience, many of them seem not to know what they are talking about.

Comparing Judaism and Islam

So how do we arrive at the truth about Islam? Is it a fundamentally violent and hateful religion, as its detractors have claimed? Or is it a religion of compassion and reason, as its Muslim adherents insist? To answer this question, we must first look inward. How have its champions and its enemies characterized Judaism? We have suffered the abuse of religious character assassination by those who not only have hated us, but also by those who have feared us. Anyone who can read is able to find excerpts in translation from the Bible and from our Talmud [Jewish oral law] and midrash [rabbinical interpretations of Jewish scriptures] that would curdle the blood of any innocent reader who doesn't know the context of the citations. Our great King David arranged the murder of an innocent man because he lusted over the poor man's wife. Rabbis incinerate their opponents. The Torah even calls for mass extermination, for genocide of the native Canaanite inhabitants of the land. It is just as easy to find violent material in the Quran and in the second most important source of Islamic religious teaching: the Hadith literature (parallel to Oral Law in Judaism). It almost need not be said that one can just as well find material urging compassion for the needy, the poor, the homeless, the orphan and widow.

Muslim "Scholars" Distort the Facts

One of my criticisms of self-proclaimed pundits of Islam is that they do not cite their sources. Take a look at some of the key issues that lie at the core of the questions listed above.

About a week before the suicide massacres and destruction of the World Trade Center towers in New York, [the television news show] *60 Minutes* claimed to have interviewed a Palestinian working for and with suicide bombers intending to kill Israelis. Interviewed in Arabic, the English voice-over translation had the man claiming that a martyr who enters Paradise will enjoy the sexual pleasures of 70 or 72 virgin women.

> **"** *One stable person's definition of suicide may be interpreted as martyrdom by a fanatic.* **"**

A number of self-proclaimed Muslim scholars accused *60 Minutes* of distorting the transcript and demanded an apology. They claimed to have heard the original Arabic in spite of the loud English voice-over and emphatically stated that he said nothing of the sort. They even went further, to claim that Islam would never teach such a thing. This was clearly an attempt to avoid public embarrassment, but the truth is that according to Islamic lore and tradition, a male who enters heaven enters what we in the West would consider a hedonistic paradise full of physical and sensual pleasures. This is simply a fact. The origin of this view most certainly lies in the context of the extremely stark and difficult life of ancient Bedouin Arabia. Something as simple as the constant flow of water in a stream was considered miraculous, so it would be natural to imagine heaven as flowing with streams of water under the shade of huge trees.

But there are other delights as well, according to a Hadith [explanation of the Quran] in an authoritative collection called *Sunan al-Tirmidhi*, which would be on the shelves of any Muslim scholar. In my edition, published in Beirut, it can be found in a section called "The Book of Description of the Garden," chapter 23, titled "The least reward for the people of Heaven," Hadith number 2562. The Hadith reads literally as follows: "Sawda (Tirmidhi's grandfather) reported that he heard from Abdullah, who received from Rishdin b. Sa'd, who in turn learned from Amr b. al-Harith, from Darraj, from Abul-Haytham, from Abu Sa'id al-Khudri, who received it from the Apostle of God [Muhammad]: The least [reward] for the people of Heaven is 80,000 servants and 72 wives, over which stands a dome of pearls, aquamarine and ruby, as [wide as the distance] between al-Jaabiyya and San'a." That these 72 wives are virgin is confirmed by Quran (55:74) and commentaries on that verse. Al-Jaabiyya was a suburb of Damascus, according to the famous 14th century commentator, Isma'il Ibn Kathir, so one personal jeweled dome would stretch the distance from Syria to Yemen, some 1,600 miles.

> *Many Muslims in the Middle East see . . . the true intent of the West [as] political and religious domination and economic exploitation.*

Was this tradition intended to be believed literally? Do Muslims believe it literally? Are they required to? This particular Hadith has technical weaknesses in its chain of transmitters and is therefore not considered impeccable, though it is listed in an authoritative collection. As a result, Muslims are not required to believe in it, though many inevitably do (but an even more respectable Hadith with virtually the same message can be found in [another authoritative collection of interpretations of the Quran,] *Tirmidhi K. Fada'il al-Jihad* [on types of holy war]

25:1663). I am sure that many believe that they will experience incredible physical pleasures when they enter heaven. I personally have no problem with that. Religions inevitably expect their adherents to believe things that would seem absurd to believers of other religions.

Suicide Bombers, Noncombatants, and Martyrdom

The more important question is, who is privileged to enter heaven according to Islam? Does a suicide bomber who kills innocent people merit entrance into heaven? The answer to this question would appear to be quite clear. Because Islam is a religious civilization that has been associated with political power for many centuries, its religious scholars have had the responsibility to deal with issues of state and with issues of war. Islam, therefore, has a lot to say on such issues. On the issue of suicide and harming innocents, Islam is unambiguous.

> *God has been hijacked by terrorists. Islam is not the problem. Terrorism is the problem.*

The four schools of Islamic law expressly forbid the harming of noncombatants. These include women, children, monks and hermits, the aged, blind and insane. In the most authoritative collection of Hadith, the *Sahih al-Bukhari* (The Book of Jihad, chapter 147, Hadiths 257–258), Muhammad expressly disapproves and then forbids the slaying of women and children. "A woman was found killed during one of the Apostle of God's battles, so the Apostle of God forbade the killing of women and children." This message is found in a number of authoritative collections and has been formalized in the legal literature. Islam also expressly forbids suicide, the punishment for which is eternal reenactment of the act and revisitation of the pain. *Sahih al-Bukhari* has the following on the authority of the Prophet: "Whoever commits suicide with a piece of iron will be punished with the same piece of iron in Hell. Whoever commits suicide by throttling shall keep on throttling himself in Hell [forever], and whoever commits suicide by stabbing shall keep on stabbing himself in Hell [forever]."

On the other hand, martyrdom in war for Islamic cause is praised extensively throughout the literature. The Quran teaches "Do not consider those killed [while engaging] in God's cause dead. Rather, they live with their Lord, who sustains them!" The Quranic idiom, "killed while engaging in God's cause" is a reference to martyrdom for acting on being a Muslim, whether as a persecuted and powerless individual or as a warrior fighting for the expansion of the world of Islam. Perhaps the most compelling expression is composed of the idioms found in the most authoritative sources and attributed to the Prophet, "Paradise is [found] under the shade of swords," or "Paradise is under the gleam of swords" (*Sahih Bukhari*, Jihad). Muhammad's companion, Abu Hurayra, said that he heard the Prophet say: "By the One in Whose hands is my soul [i.e., by God], I would love to be martyred [while engaged] in God's cause, then be resurrected, then martyred, then resurrected, then martyred, then resurrected, and then martyred." (*Sahih Bukhari*, Jihad). A Hadith in *Sunan al-Tirmidhi* states that in contrast to the suicide, the martyr does not even feel the pain of his death. He is also forgiven all his sins and has the right to intercede on behalf of his own family to enter Heaven.

A Complex Situation

So suicide is forbidden, killing of noncombatants is forbidden, but martyrdom is rewarded with entrance into heaven and, therefore, with great material rewards in the world to come. We are beginning to uncover the complexity of the problem. It rests to a great extent on interpretation and the authority of those who make the interpretations. One stable person's definition of suicide may be interpreted as martyrdom by a fanatic. All these categories may be easily manipulated by fanatical, desperate, or evil people. "A reasonable person's obvious identification of innocent noncombatants may be categorized as Satan's hordes by someone who is desperate and confused." Add to this the fact that most, though not all, suicide bombers are in desperate economic straits.

We need to add one more ingredient to an already complex soup, and this is the perception of the West (and the West includes Israel) among many Muslims who live in the Middle East. The West prides itself with having brought many gifts to the civilized world: tolerance, democracy, pluralism, freedom. To the natives of many parts of the world that were exploited by colonialism, imperialism and today's "globalism," these noble contributions are meaningless. Many Muslims in the Middle East see them as no more than slogans that attempt to hide the true intent of the West: political and religious domination and economic exploitation.

To a poor peasant or middle-class urban dweller who suffers the loss of children to disease, lacks opportunities for improvement, and has a grim and downtrodden daily existence while watching TV-movie portrayals of Western wealth and decadence, it is not a stretch to conceive of the United States and Israel as the greater and lesser Satans.

God Has Been Manipulated

Of course, local corrupt leadership often takes advantage of such sentiment in order to prop up its own crooked regimes. In fact, the secular leaders of Muslim countries have always tried to manipulate Islamic symbols and images in order to manipulate their populations. Add this also to our soup. Islam is a noble and compassionate religion, but like all good things, Islam may be cynically used and manipulated. Misguided people may also manipulate it in good faith.

The outrageously unstable political situation in the Middle East, the terrible economic situation, the lack of freedoms and lack of a tradition of open inquiry for the past six centuries all contribute to an environment of suspicion and bitterness.

Whom can you trust, if not God? But God has also been manipulated, and this is the saddest aspect of the complex we call the Middle East. God has been hijacked by terrorists. Islam is not the problem. Terrorism is the problem, and terrorists have hijacked both Islam and God.

7

The Islamic Concept of Jihad Is Comparable to the Christian Concept of Just War

Sohail H. Hashmi

Sohail H. Hashmi, who specializes in the role of Islam in international relations and the comparative ethics of war and peace, is an associate professor of international relations at Mount Holyoke College in South Hadley, Massachusetts. He was the book editor of Political Ethics: Civil Society, Pluralism, and Conflict *(2002), and the coeditor (with David Miller) of* Boundaries and Justice: Diverse Ethical Perspectives *(2001).*

According to Islam, God sanctions war as a natural and an inevitable part of human existence and gives guidance on ethical issues relating to war and peace in the Koran. The Koran states that while God's purpose for humankind is peace, violence is permissible when Islam is under attack or when the Muslim people are oppressed. In the early days of Islam, the Muslim prophet Muhammad rejected the use of military force; however, as the Muslim community began to face hostilities from the ruling tribe, Muhammad became involved in violent struggle. Islamic scholars debate whether this signaled a shift in the prophet's attitude from his previous policy of nonviolence. They also debate the original aim of jihad (holy war) and generally agree that forcible conversion to Islam was never its objective; instead, they view jihad as a powerful tool to restore political and social justice to Muslim societies. Contemporary Islamic fundamentalists declare jihad in order to combat oppression and injustice within Muslim countries and in the world. From a survey of the evolving debates on the ethics of war and peace within Islam, it is clear that the Islamic conception of jihad and the Christian conception of a just war share many principles. On the basis of this convergence, a consensus may be possible among all nations on a universal law of war and peace.

[A rab historian and philosopher] Ibn Khaldun observes in the *Muqaddima*, his celebrated introduction to a history of the world composed at the end of the fourteenth century, that "wars and different kinds of fighting have always occurred in the world since God created it." War is endemic to human existence, he writes, "something natural among human beings. No nation, and no race is free from it." Ibn Khaldun's brief comment summarizes rather well the traditional Islamic understanding of war as a universal and inevitable aspect of human existence. It is a feature of human society sanctioned, if not willed, by God Himself. The issues of war and peace thus fall within the purview of divine legislation for humanity. Islam, Muslims like to say, is a complete code of life, given the centrality of war to human existence, the moral evaluation of war holds a significant place in Muslim ethical/legal discussion." The Islamic ethics of war and peace is therefore derived from the same general sources upon which Islamic law is based.

> *Peace, not war or violence, is God's true purpose for humanity.*

The first of these sources, of course, is the Qur'an, which is held by Muslims to be God's final and definitive revelation to humanity. The Qur'anic text, like other revealed scriptures, is not a systematic treatise on ethics or law. It is a discursive commentary on the actions and experiences of the prophet Muhammad, his followers, and his opponents over the course of twenty-three years. But as the Qur'an itself argues in several verses, God's message is not limited to the time and place of its revelation; it is, rather, "a message to all the worlds" [Qur'an, verse 81:27] propounding a moral code with universal applicability. From this commentary emerge broadly defined ethical principles that have been elaborated throughout Islamic history into what may be termed an Islamic conception of divine creation and man's place in it. In other words, although the Qur'an does not present a systematic ethical argument, it is possible to derive a consistent ethical system from it.

Conceptions of War and Peace in the Qur'an

Why is humanity prone to war? The Qur'anic answer unfolds in the course of several verses revealed at various times, the essential points of which may be summarized as follows:

First, man's fundamental nature (*fitra*) is one of moral innocence, that is, freedom from sin. In other words, there is no Islamic equivalent to the notion of "original sin." Moreover, each individual is born with a knowledge of God's commandments, that is, with the essential aspects of righteous behavior. But this moral awareness is eroded as each individual encounters the corrupting influences of human society.

> *Permission [to fight] is given to those against whom War is being wrongfully waged.*

Second, man's nature is to live on the earth in a state of harmony, and peace with other living things. This is the ultimate import of the responsibility assigned by God to man as His vicegerent (*khalifa*) on this planet. True peace (*salam*) is therefore not merely an absence of war; it is the elimination of the grounds for strife or conflict, and the resulting waste and corruption (*fasad*) they create. Peace, not war or violence, is God's true purpose for humanity.

Third, given man's capacity for wrongdoing, there will always be some who *choose* to violate their nature and transgress against God's commandments. Adam becomes fully human only when he chooses to heed Iblis's (Satan's) temptation and disobeys God. As a result of this initial act of disobedience, human beings are expelled from the Garden to dwell on earth as "enemies to each other" [Qur'an, verses 2:36 and 7:24]. Thus, wars and the evils that stem from them, the Qur'an suggests, are the inevitable consequences of the uniquely human capacity for moral choice.

> *Throughout the Meccan period . . . [the Prophet's] policy can only be described as nonviolent resistance.*

The Qur'an does not present the fall of man as irrevocable, however, for God quickly returns to Adam to support and guide him. This, according to Islamic belief, is the beginning of continuous divine revelation to humanity through a series of prophets ending with Muhammad. God's reminders of the laws imprinted upon each human consciousness through His prophets are a manifestation of His endless mercy to His creation, because all human beings are potential victims of Iblis's guile, that is, potential evildoers, and most human beings are actually quite far from God's laws. When people form social units, they become all the more prone to disobey God's laws through the obstinate persistence in wrongdoing caused by custom and social pressures. In this way, the individual drive for power, wealth, prestige, and all the other innumerable human goals becomes amplified. Violence is the inevitable result of the human desire for self-aggrandizement.

Permission for Defensive Jihad

Fourth, each prophet encounters opposition from those (always a majority) who persist in their rebellion against God, justifying their actions through various self-delusions. One of the principal characteristics of rejection of God (*kufr*) is the inclination toward violence and oppression, encapsulated by the broad concept *zulm*. When individuals choose to reject divine guidance, either by transgressing against specific divine injunctions or by losing faith altogether, they violate . . . their own nature (*fitra*). When Adam and Eve disobey the divine command in the Garden, the Qur'an relates that they cry out in their despair not that they have sinned against God, but that they have transgressed against their own souls. When an entire society rejects God, oppression and violence become the norm throughout the society and in relation with other societies as well the moral anarchy that prevails when human beings abandon the higher moral code derived from faith in a supreme and just Creator, the Qur'an suggests, is fraught with potential and actual violence.

Fifth, peace (salam) is attainable only when beings surrender to God's will and live according to God's laws. This is the condition of *islam*, the conscious decision to acknowledge in faith and conduct the presence and power of God. Because human nature is not sufficiently strong to resist the temptation to evil, it is necessary for man to establish a human agency, that is, a state, to mitigate the effects of anarchy and enforce divine law.

> *In Medina . . . the Muslims became a coherent community, and . . . the Prophet enacted a new policy . . . aimed at redressing Muslim grievances.*

Sixth, because it is unlikely that individuals or societies will ever conform fully to the precepts of Islam, Muslims must always be prepared to fight to preserve the Muslim faith and Muslim principles. The use of force by the Muslim community is, therefore, sanctioned by God as a necessary response to the existence of evil in the world. As the Qur'an elaborates in an early revelation, the believers are those "who, whenever tyranny afflicts them, defend themselves." This theme of the just, God-ordained use of force for legitimate purposes is continued in several other verses. In the first verse that explicitly permits the Muslim community to use armed force against its enemies, the Qur'an makes clear that fighting is a burden imposed upon all believers (not only Muslims) as a result of the enmity harbored by the unbelievers.

Permission [to fight] is given to those against whom War is being wrongfully waged, and verily, God has indeed the power to succor them: those who have been driven from their homelands against all right for no other reason than their saying: "Our Sustainer is God!" For, if God had not enabled people to defend themselves against one another, monasteries and churches and synagogues and mosques—in all of which God's name is abundantly extolled—would surely have been destroyed.

A subsequent verse converts this permission to fight into an injunction: The rationale given for using armed force is quite explicit "Tumult and oppression (*fitna*) is worse than killing" [Qur'an, verse 2:19]. These two verses clearly undermine the possibility of an Islamic pacifism. One verse in particular offers an implicit challenge to an ethical position based on the renunciation of all violence: "Fighting is prescribed for you, even though it be hateful to you; but it may well be that you hate something that is in fact good for you, and that you love a thing that is in fact bad for you: and God knows, whereas you do not" [Qur'an, verse 2:216]. There is, thus, no equivalent in the Islamic tradition of the continuing debate within Christianity of the possibility of just war: There is no analogue in Islamic texts to [thirteenth-century Italian Christian philosopher Thomas] Aquinas's Question 40: "Are some wars permissible?" The Islamic discourse on war and peace begins from the a priori assumption that some types of war are permissible—indeed, required by God—and that all other forms of violence are, therefore, forbidden. In short, the Qur'an's attitude toward war and peace may be described as an idealistic realism. Human existence is characterized neither by incessant warfare nor by real peace, but by a continuous tension between the two. Societies exist forever in a precarious balance between them. The unending human challenge *jihad fi sabil Allah* (struggle in the way of God) to mitigate the possibility of war to strengthen the grounds for peace. The resulting human condition may bear out the truth of the angels' initial protest to God that his decision to create man will only lead to corruption and bloodshed in the world. But the Qur'anic message is, if anything, continually optimistic about "the human capacity to triumph over evil. God silences the angels, after all, not by denying their prognostication, but by holding out the possibility of unforeseen potential: 'I know what you know not' [Qur'an, verse 2:30].". . .

Muhammad's Approach to War and Peace

We can construct an outline of the Prophet's approach to the ethics of war and peace not only by referring to the Qur'an, but also by making use of the large body of literature comprising the Prophet's sayings and actions (*hadith*) and biography (*sira*) compiled between the second and fourth Islamic centuries. It is clear from these records that from an early age, Muhammad was averse to many aspects of the tribal culture in which he was born. In particular, there is no indication that he ever showed any interest in affairs of tribal honor, particularly in the ghazwa [skirmishes among neighboring tribes], throughout the Meccan period of his prophetic mission (610–22 C.E.), he showed no inclination toward the use of force in any form, even for self-defense—on the contrary, his policy can only be described as nonviolent resistance. This policy was maintained in spite of escalating physical attacks directed at his followers and at him personally. And it was maintained in spite of growing pressure from within the Muslim ranks to respond in kind, particularly after the conversion of two men widely considered to embody traditional Arab virtues, the Prophet's uncle Hamza and 'Umar ibn al-Khattab. Some Qur'anic verses reflect the growing tension among the Meccan Muslims over the use of force. Nevertheless, the Prophet insisted throughout this period on the virtues of patience and steadfastness in the face of their opponents' attacks. When the persecution of the most vulnerable Muslims (former slaves and members of Mecca's poorer families) became intense, he directed them to seek refuge in the realm of a Christian king, Abyssinia. The Prophet's rejection of armed struggle during the Meccan period was more than mere prudence based on the Muslims' military weakness. It was, rather, derived from the Qur'an's still unfolding conception that the use of force should be avoided unless it is, in just war parlance, a "last resort." This ethical perspective is clearly outlined in the continuation of a verse cited earlier, which defines the believers as those who defend themselves when oppressed.

Jihad Meant Nonviolent Resistance

The requital of evil is an evil similar to it hence, whoever pardons [his enemy] and makes peace, his reward rests with God—for, verily, He does not love evildoers. Yet indeed, as for any who defend themselves after having been wronged—no blame whatever attaches to them: blame attaches but to those who oppress [other] people and behave outrageously on earth, offending against all right: for them is grievous suffering in store! But if one is patient in adversity and forgives, this is indeed the best resolution of affairs.

The main result of these early verses is not to reaffirm the pre-Islamic custom of lex talionis [law of retaliation, or "an eye for an eye"] but the exact opposite: to establish the moral superiority of forgiveness over revenge. The permission of self-defense is not a call to arms; military force is not mentioned, although neither is it proscribed. Instead, it should be seen as a rejection of quietism, of abnegation of moral responsibility in the face of oppression. Active nonviolent resistance and open defiance of pagan persecution is the proper Muslim response, according to these verses, and was, in fact, the Prophet's own practice during this period. Because the Meccan period of the Prophet's mission lasted almost fourteen years, three years longer than the Medinan period, it is absolutely fundamental in the construction of an Islamic ethical system. Clearly, jihad in this extended period of the Prophet's life meant nonviolent resistance. For potential Muslim nonviolent activists, there are many lessons to be learned from the Prophet's decisions during these years. But, regrettably, the Meccan period has received scant attention, either from Muslim activists or from jurists, historians, and moralists.

Jihad Acquires Military Focus

The period that has been the traditional focus of Muslim and non-Muslim concern in discussing the Islamic approach to war and peace is the decade during which the prophet lived in Medina (622–32 C.E.). It was in Medina that the Muslims became a coherent community, and it was here that jihad acquired its military component. According to the early Muslim historians, the Prophet enacted a new policy toward the Quraysh, the ruling tribe of Mecca, within a year of settling Medina aimed at redressing Muslim grievances. He authorized small raids against specific pagan targets, in particular caravans proceeding along the trade route to Syria. These raids, according to many orientalist accounts, were intended specifically to be a means of collecting booty in order to alleviate the financial distress of the immigrants, to Medina as well as to provide an added incentive for potential converts. The raids, it is suggested, signaled a fundamental shift in the Prophet's approach to an emphasis upon violent struggle, a shift sanctioned by increasingly belligerent Qur'anic verses of the Medinan period. Both the early historians' accounts and the subsequent orientalist speculations have been challenged by contemporary Muslim biographers of the Prophet. Muhammad Haykal [in *The Life of Muhammad* (1976)], for example, argues that the early forays were not military expeditions but only small raids intended to harass the Meccans, impress upon them the new power of the Muslims, and demonstrate the necessity for a peace accommodation with the Muslims.

Both positions in the debate are obviously speculative. The

uncertainty regarding any shift in the Prophet's attitude toward the employment of violence is compounded by the uncertainty regarding the actual date of the Qur'anic revelation permitting fighting. Haykal himself implies that the Qur'anic permission to fight had already been revealed before these expeditions: "This peaceful show of strength by Islam does not all mean that Islam, at that time, forbade fighting in defense of personal life and religion, or to put a stop to persecution. What it did really mean at that time, as it does today or will ever do, was to condemn any war of aggression.". . .

Debates on the Grounds for War

The medieval juristic literature is characterized by fundamental disagreements on the grounds for war. But most of the legal scholars agree that the object of jihad is not the forcible conversion of unbelievers to the Islamic faith. This object would contradict several clear Qur'anic statements enjoining freedom of worship, including "Let there be no compulsion in religion; the truth stands out clearly from error," [verse 2:256] and "If your Lord had so willed, all those who are on earth would have believed: you then compel mankind, against their will, to believe?" [verse 10:99] With regard to verse 9:5, which seems to sanction a war of mass conversion of all polytheists to Islam, most acknowledge that the full context in which the verse occurs limits its application to the pagan Arabs who were so implacably opposed to the earliest Muslim community at Medina. The object of jihad is generally held by these writers to be the subjugation of hostile powers who refuse to permit the preaching of Islam, not forcible conversion. Once under Muslim rule, they reason, non-Muslims will be free to consider the merits of Islam. The medieval theory of an ongoing jihad, and the bifurcation of the world into dar al-Islam and dar al-harb[1] upon which it was predicated, became a fiction soon after it was elaborated by medieval writers. The "house of Islam" disintegrated into a number of rival states, some of whom found themselves allied with states belonging to the "house of war" in fighting their co-religionists. Nevertheless, the idea that "Islam" and the "West" represented monolithic and mutually antagonistic civilizations underlay much Muslim and European writing, partic-

---

1. Dar al-Islam means land of Islam or land of peace. Dar al-harb means land of war, referring to all areas that are not dar al-Islam.

ularly during the heyday of European imperialism in the eighteenth and nineteenth centuries. Shades of this viewpoint are very much apparent in our own day. . . .

Contemporary Islamic Fundamentalists Wage War for Social Justice

With the emergence of postcolonial Muslim states, political legitimacy and the rights of the people in the face of oppressive regimes have emerged as central issues in Islamic discourse. These issues figure prominently, of course, in all fundamentalist literature. Fundamentalists view themselves as a vanguard of the righteous, preparing the way for the elimination of jahili [corrupt, irreligious, Western] values from their societies and the establishment of a just "Islamic" order. The details of this order remain vague in the fundamentalist tracts. What is clear from these works is the view, supported by experience, that the secular, nationalist regimes ruling most Muslim countries today, backed by their Western supporters, will not willingly cede power, even if the majority of the population does not support them. They will maintain power by any means, including the violent repression of dissent. In other words, it is argued that these regimes have declared war on Islam within their countries, and that it is incumbent upon all true believers to respond by whatever means are necessary, including violence, to overthrow them. The fundamentalist writings are therefore focused on combating the social and international oppression that they believe face the Muslim community (*umma*) everywhere. Jihad is for the fundamentalists an instrument for the realization of political and social justice in their own societies, a powerful tool for internal reform and one required by the Qur'an's command that Muslims "enjoin the right and forbid the wrong." The thrust of the modern jihad is thus very much inward. Warfare on the international level is considered only to the extent that Western governments are viewed as archenemies who impose corrupt and authoritarian regimes upon Muslims. Jihad as an instrument for the imposition of Islamic rule in non-Muslim states today hardly figures in fundamentalists' works. That goal has been postponed indefinitely, given the fundamentalist position, which they share with many other Muslim writers, that most of the Muslim countries themselves do not at present have Islamic governments. . . .

Debates on Right Conduct in War

Because the goal of jihad is the call to Islam; not territorial conquest or plunder, the right conduct of Muslim armies has traditionally been an important concern within Islam. The Qur'an provides the basis for *ius in bello* [laws governing conduct in war] considerations: "And fight in God's cause against those who wage war against you, but do not transgress limits, for God loves not the transgressors" [Qur'an verse 2:190]. The "limits" are enumerated in the practice of the Prophet and the first four caliphs. According to authoritative traditions, whenever the Prophet sent out a military force, he would instruct its commander to adhere to certain restraints. The Prophet's immediate successors continued this practice, as is indicated by the "ten commands" of the first caliph, Abu Bakr:

> Do not act treacherously; do not act disloyally; do not act neglectfully. Do not mutilate; do not kill little children or old men, or women; do not cut off the heads of the palm-trees or burn them; do not cut down the fruit tress; do not slaughter a sheep or a cow or a camel, except for food. You will pass by people who devote their lives in cloisters; leave them and their devotions alone. You will come upon people who bring you platters in which are various sorts of food; if you eat any of it, mention the name of God over it.

Thus, the Qur'an and the actions of the Prophet and his successors established . . . [the broad principles of the right conduct in war. Medieval jurists, however, were divided about] a number of issues raised by the Qur'an itself: the treatment of prisoners, both combatants and noncombatants; the granting of quarter or safe passage (*aman*) to residents of dar al-harb and the division of booty. In addition, the jurists also dealt with the traditional concerns of *ius in bello:* the definition and protection of noncombatants and restrictions on certain types of weapon. The legal discussions address three issues: Who is subject to damage in war? What types of damage may be inflicted upon persons? What types of damage may be inflicted upon their property? Underlying the differing opinions on these issues once again are the apparent contradictions between the peace verses and the sword verses. The jurists who contend that the sword verses provide a general rule superseding earlier revelation argue that belief is the decisive factor in establishing immunity from attack. Since verse 9:5, in their view, commands Muslims to fight all polytheists, only women and children (who were specifically designated by the Prophet as immune) are prohibited targets. All able-bodied polytheist males, whether actually fighting or not, may be killed.

> *The object of jihad is generally held . . . to be the subjugation of hostile powers who refuse to permit the preaching of Islam, not forcible conversion.*

Other jurists, who do not consider the peace verses to have been abrogated, maintain that capacity to fight is the only appropriate consideration, and therefore include old men, women, children, peasants, slaves, and hermits among prohibited targets. The prohibition against direct attack, however, does not establish the absolute immunity of noncombatants, because, according to most jurists, all of these persons (except for hermits) are subject to the laws pertaining to prisoners of war. . . .

Islamic Jihad and Western Just War

Is the Islamic jihad the same as the Western just war? The answer, of course, depends upon who is defining the concepts. But after this brief survey of the debates that have historically surrounded the Islamic approach to war and peace and the controversies that are continuing to this day, I think it is safe to conclude that even though jihad may not be identical to the just war as it has evolved in the West, the similarities between Western and Islamic thinking on war and peace are far more numerous than the differences.

Jihad, the just war, was conceived by its early theorists basically as a means to circumscribe the legitimate reasons for war so that peace is inevitably enhanced. Jihad, like just war, is grounded in the belief that intersocietal relations should be peaceful, not marred by constant and destructive warfare. The surest way for human beings to realize this peace is for them to obey the divine law that is imprinted on the human conscience and therefore accessible to everyone, believers and unbelievers. According to the medieval law, Muslims are obliged to propagate this divine law, through peaceful means if possible, through violent means if necessary. No war was jihad unless it was undertaken with right intent and as a last resort, and declared by right authority. Most Muslims today disavow the duty to propagate Islam by force and limit jihad to self-defense. And finally, jihad, like just war, places strict limitations on legitimate targets during war and demands that belligerents use the least amount of force necessary to achieve the swift cessation of hostilities. Both jihad and just war are dynamic concepts, still evolving and adapting to changing international realities. As Muslims continue to interpret the Islamic ethics of war and peace, their debates on jihad will, I believe, increasingly parallel the Western debates on just war. And as Muslims and non-Muslims continue their recently begun dialogue on the just international order, they may well find a level of agreement on the ethics of war and peace that will ultimately be reflected in a revised and more universal law of war and peace.

8

The Islamic Concept of Jihad Differs from the Christian Concept of Just War

Jean Flori

Jean Flori, a specialist in the history of ideologies, is director of research at France's National Research Council in Paris. He is author of several books about the Crusades and holy war.

From its inception, Islam encouraged the waging of war against Christians and Jews and glorified those who gave their lives to conquer people of other faiths. Both the Koran and the prophet Muhammad promoted jihad. In contrast, Jesus of Nazareth was a pacifist and the teachings of the Gospel oppose violence and war. Only a thousand years after Jesus's death did the Christian doctrine of holy war emerge when Christians sought to defend themselves against attacks by Muslims. President Bush's declaration of a "war on terror," in which he described the military action as a "crusade," has greatly provoked many Muslims who believe that the West is deliberately trying to destroy Islam.

O n 11 September 2001, the collapse of the twin towers of New York's World Trade Center, broadcast live to every television screen, brutally brought the ambiguous notion of jihad [Muslim holy war] to the Western world's attention.

It's a worrying notion indeed: in the attackers' parlance, it

Jean Flori, "Jihad and Holy War," *Queen's Quarterly*, vol. 110, Fall 2003, p. 339. Copyright © 2003 by Jean Flori. Reproduced by permission.

seems to mean simply the first episodes of a holy war waged in the name of God against "Jews and Crusaders," who are taken to be responsible for the oppression of the Muslim world. This jihad is held to be holy and meritorious: those who die as martyrs in the fight for the cause of Islam gain eternal life. Commanded by God, its ultimate success is assured; this is why [Osama] bin Laden is quick to predict the failure of the United States and the Western world, and the definitive triumph of Islam. The Palestinian kamikazes speak the same language: they too are certain that they will reach a martyr's paradise.

For most Westerners, immersed as they have been for generations in a culture that has undergone a "secular revolution," this kind of discourse seems to come from an age long past, and even in learned orientalist circles it is common to dismiss it with a shrug, as though it were representative of only a tiny minority of inflamed, deranged or demented fanatics. But in most Muslim countries, one need only listen to the people on the street to be convinced of quite the opposite. There, it is obvious that the "secular revolution" has not taken place, and it is far from certain that it will come about in the foreseeable future. The idea of praiseworthy violent jihad shocks no one. In contrast, so-called "moderate" Muslims, especially those who live in Western countries, try to marginalize or minimize the phenomenon. They rightly underline Islam's positive cultural aspects, for instance its traditional tolerance of other faiths, expressly forbidding forcible conversions which through the whole of the Middle Ages made possible the relatively peaceful coexistence of Muslims and the dhimmi (Christians and Jews) who were allowed to live in Islamic lands under Muslim domination. Furthermore, the "moderates" are careful to represent Islam as a religion of peace, and jihad as an "effort in the ways of God" with essentially peaceful connotations.

A History of Violent Jihad in Islam

But this attempt, while morally admirable, still runs against historical reality: even if it is indeed true that the word "jihad" does not always mean violent action and cannot be systematically translated as "holy war," it is nevertheless equally true that the warlike dimension is included in nearly two thirds of jihad's occurrences in the Koran. In other words, jihad is not equivalent to holy war, but holy war is a major component of jihad, and this has been so since the earliest origins of Islam.

Indeed, in contrast to Jesus, who condemned the use of violence and weapons, the Prophet Mohammed personally took part in a number of armed expeditions, commanding a few himself and preaching in favour of even more; he balked neither at pillage, nor at political assassination, nor at the massacre of prisoners who were not worth holding for ransom. Many Koranic texts sanction the use of armed violence, and authentic Muslim tradition, both in the "sayings" of the Prophet (Sunna) and in the story of his life (Sira), shows that right from Islam's origins death in battle under jihad would guarantee a martyr's glory and his entry into Paradise.

> *In most Muslim countries . . . the idea of praiseworthy violent jihad shocks no one.*

The doctrine of warlike jihad, codified by ninth-century lawmakers, therefore has its roots both in the Koran and in the life and sayings of the Prophet. This is to say that, from the beginning, Islam shows no moral reluctance in using force of arms and in making holy a war waged for the sake of the Muslim community. Such war is not waged to convert monotheistic infidels, but rather to extend the "house of Islam" through the conquest of the infidels' territory (i.e., the "house of war"), a conquest likened to a "liberation from unbelief." War thus waged contributes to the ultimate, definitive, and inexorable victory of the Muslim community (Umma). Warlike jihad is therefore, and from the beginning, validated and sanctified both by written revelation and the Prophet's actions.

Christianity Is Based on Radical Pacifism

The same cannot be said of Christianity, precisely because of its founder's radically pacifist attitude. Jesus of Nazareth rejected any use of force and of weapons to establish his kingdom or to ensure the success of his message. His earliest disciples imitated him, preferring to die by the sword than use it for any reason whatever. The "Christian martyr" is thus by definition the peaceful and pacifist victim of an armed violence that he completely rejects. Even into the third century, the Roman Church would allow a soldier to become a Christian only if he would refuse to kill, even if ordered to do so by his superiors. Christians themselves were barred from becoming soldiers.

This radical pacifism was gradually loosened over time, in the interests of defending a Roman Empire that had become Christian early in the fourth century. Even then, so-called "just" war was tolerated only as a necessary evil designed to prevent still greater evil. It was given no positive moral worth, and soldiers who, under orders, killed the enemy on the battlefield were no less subject to penitence. It is only in the middle of the ninth century that the first text emerges to allow spiritual rewards for warriors fighting for the pope, threatened in Rome by Muslim raiding parties. But in the eleventh century, a century marked by the reconquest of formerly Christian territories (in Spain, Sicily, and the Near East) that had fallen into Islamic hands, Christianity began to work out a real doctrine of holy war. This doctrine culminated in the First Crusade, preached by Pope Urban II in 1095: Christian warriors were told that their sins would be forgiven if they fought for the liberation of Christ's tomb at Jerusalem, at the time the principal destination for pilgrims.

> *From the beginning, Islam shows no moral reluctance in using force of arms . . . for the sake of the Muslim community.*

The expedition's twofold goal of reconquest and pilgrimage bestowed a double spiritual privilege: to the one that had always been attached to pilgrimage (the forgiveness of one's confessed sins) was added the privilege of a martyr's crown for those who died in a "holy war," a concept now on its way to being defined. It is therefore at this time, over a thousand years after the death of Jesus, that the Christian doctrine of holy war connects with Muslim jihad.

Differences Between Islamic Jihad and Christian Holy War

There are, however, three significant subtleties.

First, warlike jihad is allowed and valued right from the beginnings of Islam: it is permitted by the Koran and by the founder's actions. For Christianity, by contrast, holy war is completely contrary to the principles of the Gospel and to the acts of Jesus. It is the result of a slow historical evolution, culminating in the Christian doctrine of holy war.

Second, jihad is a war of conquest/liberation of territory that was not previously subject to the laws of Islam. A crusade is, on the contrary, a war of reconquest of territory still largely populated by Christians and which was the ancient cradle of Christianity.

Third, jihad is meant to extend Islam's territory outward from its holy places, Mecca, Medina, and Jerusalem. Crusades were preached in order to reconquer Jerusalem and Christ's tomb, first among Christianity's holy places and far ahead of Rome and Santiago de Compostela. Its degree of holiness for Christians was such that the mission to recapture it is comparable to a jihad that would be undertaken to free Mecca itself from occupation by the infidel.

It is nevertheless true that the reconquest was, and remains, perceived by the Muslims as an intolerable act of aggression. In the collective Muslim mind, it left a kind of painful wound that has been the cause of deep bitterness. It is seen as the first "colonization" of the Muslim world by the Christian West.

Awakening Violent Forms of Jihad

It is for this reason that the declaration of a "war on terror" by President George W. Bush, uttered a few hours after the 11 September attack, doubly disturbed many a Muslim mind. The extremely unfortunate use of the term "crusade" for the military/police action to come against the terrorist "sanctum" in Taliban-controlled Afghanistan is a political mistake that bears witness to a deep lack of historical understanding and to a deliberate disregard for non-American mentalities. This extraordinary gaffe, reinforced by a regrettable reference to Wild West justice ("wanted, dead or alive"), has reinforced even further a conviction—throughout the Muslim world—that the West pursues a deliberate policy of aggression against Islam. It is a conviction that has grown stronger, as the war against Iraq can only validate, and will therefore serve to strengthen the awakening of the ever-living but until now dormant, notion of jihad in its most violent form.

9

The Muslim Prophet Muhammad Was a Gentle and Compassionate Man

Akbar S. Ahmed

Akbar S. Ahmed is a professor of Islamic studies at the American University in Washington, D.C. Acknowledged as one of the foremost authorities on Islam in America, Ahmed has written many books, including Islam Today: A Short Introduction to the Islamic World *(1998) and* Islam Under Siege: Living Dangerously in a Post-Honor World *(2003).*

In the seventh century, on the windy peaks of Mount Hira in Saudi Arabia, the Muslim prophet Muhammad was instructed by God in the teachings of the new religion of Islam. The philosophy of Islam emphasized peace, and the prophet Muhammad had a kind and gentle nature and showed no inclination toward violence. His life served as a model of the ideals and principles of Islam, including a belief in a universal humanity that transcends caste, class, and nationality. The Islamic ideal also emphasizes promoting understanding and peace among different groups of people.

There is no better way to discover Islam than to climb Mount Hira, a few miles from Makkah [in Saudi Arabia]. The ascent provides insights into the nature of Islam and its Prophet. On the bleak top the winds blow with ferocity, creat-

Akbar S. Ahmed, *Discovering Islam: Making Sense of Muslim History and Society.* New York: Routledge, 2002. First published 1988 by Routledge & Kegan Paul Ltd.

ing a sense of elemental power, exactly as it must have been in the seventh century. The place speaks of a man looking for solitude, of a man searching for answers. Here the Prophet suffered the agony of rejecting an old religion, and experienced the ecstasy of discovering a new one. There is nothing man-made on the peak. Abruptly loneliness, then awe, and finally exaltation fill the heart. In the most profound sense one is face to face with oneself.

The cave, the Prophet's refuge, is tiny. It points to Makkah and the *haram sharif* [holy sanctuary] containing the Kaaba [central shrine of Islam], is faintly visible. The drop from the cave is sheer, about 2,000 feet. The climb itself is steep. I, not much older than the Prophet when he received the call to Islam at 40, was stiff the next day. Praying on the spot, in the cave, where Islam was revealed is highly evocative for a Muslim. Away from the crowds, from the signs of our age, Mount Hira is a unique experience—one of the most exhilarating of my life.

When the Prophet was about 40, in 610, on a retreat on Mount Hira he saw a vision. This was the first call. It came in the form of an angel ordering him to read—*iqra*—(hence Quran, reading). 'Read', commanded the angel. Frightened, the Prophet stammered, 'I do not read'. Twice more the angel ordered him to read and the third time replied: 'Read in the name of your Lord, the Creator, who created man of a clot of blood. Read. Your Lord is most gracious. It is He who taught man by the pen that which he does not know.' The Quran was then revealed to him.

The Prophet was the culmination of a long line of prophets —124,000 of them—many no more than good, exemplary people. He was the last, the seal, of the prophets, the final messenger of God. The prophets did not claim divinity. They were humans entrusted by God to spread the word. The Prophet of Islam had brought the Quran which was, like him, final and cumulative.

The Quran

The holy Quran is a collection of divinely inspired utterances and discourses. It is a book of some 300 pages divided into 114 chapters called Surahs. These are arranged roughly in order of length except for the short and popular prayer which constitutes Surah 1, *Al Fatihah*, the opening; Surah 2, *Al Baqarah*, the cow, has 286 verses; Surah 3, *Al Imran*, the family of Imran, has 200; Surah 4, *An Nisa*, women, has 177, and so on down to the final Surahs which have only 3–6 short verses. As the Madinan [Surahs or sayings made in Madinah] are generally the longer ones the order is not chronological. The formula *'Bismillah ar-Rahman ar-Rahim'*, 'in the name of Allah, the Beneficent, the Merciful', is prefixed to every Surah except one.

For our purposes—to explore an ideal of social behaviour—Surah 17, *Al Isra*, the children of Israel, is important. It reflects those aspects of the Prophet's social behaviour we are emphasizing. Be kind to parents, kin, the poor and the wayfarer, exhorts the Surah. Do not be a spend-thrift, kill, commit adultery or cheat, it warns. Boasting and false pride are condemned and honesty lauded. When humans err, and if they are sincere, 'God forgives those who repent'.

> *Forgiveness and compassion are presupposed in the ninety-nine names of Allah.*

The general tone of the holy Quran is sombre and meditative. It is a dialogue between God and humanity. At the core is a moral earnestness. Because it is not an academic thesis it needs no structure, no order, no introduction and conclusion. It is a vibrant outpouring of divine messages, of powerful bursts reflecting different moods. It warns, advises and exhorts in flashes. The Quranic impulses, arriving like claps of thunder, cover the entire gamut of life. Its language is eloquent, its imagery awesome; its scope is humankind and no less. Man and woman are given the highest possible status, that of vicegerent of God on earth. The Quran repeatedly points them to knowledge: *ilm* is the second most used word in the Quran after the name of God. Human beings are told to use their mind and think in at least 300 places.

Forgiveness and compassion are presupposed in the ninety-nine names of Allah contained in the Quran. If we divided the ninety-nine names into those with positive attributes—truth, justice, mercy and compassion—and those with negative ones—suggesting anger and retribution—we would have only four or five in the second category. When man errs Allah is indeed *Muntaqim* (the Avenger). But along with being the Avenger Allah is also *al-Afu* (the Pardoner) and *at-Tawab* (the Accepter of repentance).

Above all, Allah is *ar-Rahman*, the Beneficent, and *ar-Rahim*, the Merciful. By containing these two attributes the common Muslim recitation, *Bismillah ar-Rahman ar-Rahim*, underlines their significance in understanding Allah. In addition, Allah is *al-Mohaymin*, the Protector, *al-Ghaffar*, the Forgiver, *ar-Razzaq*, the Provider, and *al-Ghafur*, the All-Forgiving. Allah is also the Just, *al-Adl*, representing the Truth, *al-Haq*, the Source of All Goodness, *al-Barr*, and the Light, *an-Noor.*

> **❝** *Muslim prayers can create sublimity around the believer, peace within.* **❞**

Allah emerges as generous and compassionate. Humanity has been created by Allah and therefore Allah understands its weaknesses. And because Allah is dealing with human beings who are sometimes fickle and sometimes uncertain Allah is *as-Sabur*, Patient. In Allah humans find the source of peace, *as-Salam*, for Allah is Loving, *al-Wadud*, and Wise, *al-Hakim.*

The Essence of Islam

The five 'pillars'—obligatory duties—of Islam sum up its essence: *tauhid*, faith in one God, unity; *salat*, the daily prayers, a constant reminder of the transitory nature of life and *tauhid*; *sawm*, fasting during the month of Ramadan to develop moral and physical discipline; the annual *zakat* to re-distribute wealth to the poorer sections of society; and *haj*, the pilgrimage, once in a lifetime, to be part of the annual congregation of Muslims in Makkah. Islamic ritual emphasized unity among the Muslim community, the brotherhood, the *ummah*; its philosophy emphasized peace, *salaam* (hence Islam).

Islam's appeal lay—and lies—in its simplicity: one God, one Book, one Prophet. It was a tidy, uncomplicated religion with clearly defined ritual. But the simplicity was deceptive. Layers of profundity covered it. As a boy I thought the five daily prayers were meant to instil discipline—the regular washing and waking at early hours in preparation for prayers and the bowing and bending during them. Later, in manhood, I gradually perceived the deeper significance of the prayers. They were a constant reminder of the transient, passing nature of the world. And, related to this, a constant declaration of the permanence of Allah. Muslim prayers can create sublimity around the believer, peace within.

The Muslim ideal rests on the important Quranic concepts of *al-adl*, equilibrium, and *al-ahsan*, compassion. A life based on these is a balanced one. Islam is a religion of balance, equilibrium, of the middle. The Islamic virtues are courage, generosity, cleanliness and piety; and in his life the Prophet exemplifies them. . . .

The Prophet's Gentle Nature

For the twentieth-century imagination a Biblical prophet is someone from a Cecil B. De Mille film. A towering, fierce figure he is wont to thunder, which he does often and long, about hell and damnation, while his eyes blaze and his wild, flowing, white beard bristles with frenzy. It is wise not to cross him; he can convert a staff into a snake with ease and, when pressed, part the waves in the sea. Our Prophet, then, the last in the line of the Semitic prophets, the seal of all prophets, must be an even more imposing and fearsome figure, it may reasonably be conjectured. Nothing is further from the truth.

Piety, forbearance, courage and judgment—required in some degree by any leader—the Prophet had, and displayed, in abundance. But what is striking about his behaviour and temperament is the most unexpected quality in tribal life, gentleness. It is a quality the critics of Islam overlook and its supporters take for granted; the omission partly explains why images of Islam as a religion of hate and rage flourish.

> *" What is striking about [the Prophet's] behaviour and temperament is . . . gentleness. "*

Whether consoling a child who lost an animal, or not being able to control his tears when breaking bad news to the wife of a friend, or requesting that the bitch which had delivered puppies be kept warm, or telling Aishah 'softly and gently please' when she was rough to an obstinate camel, this aspect of the man emerges. Added to the gentleness was a distinct vein of humour, a capacity to smile at the incongruous and unexpected. Upbraiding Abu Bakr—'look at this pilgrim'—for being harsh to a camel on a pilgrimage or the lifting of a serious mood with Aishah's suggestion that if she died he would feel no remorse and after the burial immediately take another wife, this trait of the Prophet inspired devotion and love. It would make him, in the words of the Quran, 'a mercy to the worlds'.

> *Harshness and violence were simply not part of the Prophet's nature.*

The gentle affection for the weak in society—women, children, orphans—may have sprung from the Prophet's own childhood. His father, Abdullah, died before his birth and his mother Aminah, when he was six. His grandfather, in whose charge he was left, died when he was eight. His last public address at Arafat advises Muslims to 'treat your women well and be kind to them'. 'Paradise', he thrice repeated to a questioner who wished to find a short cut to heaven, 'lies under the feet of the mother.' In early Islamic history Khadijah and Aishah, his wives, and Fatimah, his daughter, play important roles.

The Prophet's Kindness to Women

The Prophet's kindness to women forms the content of many stories. One concerns his wife, Maria, the Christian Coptic slave girl, sent to him by the head of the Coptic church in Cairo. His attentiveness towards her had provoked his other wives into arguments and bad temper. They made life unbearable for him. In protest he withdrew from them for a month, sleeping on the floor of a small, mud store-room and refusing to see anyone. Umar, when he finally succeeded in seeing him, broke into a cry of anguish, threatening to cut off his own daughter's head for having brought the Prophet to this point. But by now the women had learnt a lesson. They promised there would be harmony in the home if he came back. Another man in those times and in that society would have been excused for taking the cane to his wives.

The Prophet's gentleness presupposed a forgiving and tolerant nature. This is confirmed by historical—and momentous—examples. Hind, the implacable foe of Islam . . ., in a gesture of hatred and contempt, ate the raw liver of Hamzah, a hero of Badr and brother of the Prophet's father. It was widely assumed that the Prophet would never forgive her. Hamzah was one of his dearest relatives (and destined to be a favourite Muslim hero in distant parts of the world. When Makkah was finally conquered and Hind taken captive the Prophet forgave her. Overwhelmed by his generosity she became a Muslim, declaring he must be a prophet and no ordinary mortal (her progeny would reap the dividends: Muawiyah, her son, founded the Umayyad dynasty).

> *One of the main contributions of Islam was the concept of universalistic humanity transcending tribe and clan.*

After the conquest of Makkah the Prophet announced a general amnesty. Those who had abused, humiliated and injured him were forgiven, much to the chagrin of those Muslims thirsting for revenge. The conquest of Makkah cost less than 30 lives. The final victory of Islam—comparable in historical significance to the great revolutions, French, Russian and Chinese—is the cheapest in terms of human life.

The charge of those critics who accuse the Prophet of the deaths of a poet who wrote satirical verse and of the Quraiza, a Jewish tribe of Madinah, will not hold. An over-zealous Muslim infuriated by his verses set out to silence the poet in the first case. In the second the arbiter chosen by the Quraiza condemned their fighting men to death—or apostasy—for breaking a treaty in a critical battle which almost destroyed the entire early Muslim community. Harshness and violence were simply not part of the Prophet's nature. Yet on religious matters he was firm and unequivocal, showing no vacillation or doubt.

The Prophet's Humility and Ethics

Along with the virtues of gentleness and tolerance his behaviour exemplified that of humility. Once he was persuading a leading Quraysh aristocrat to become a Muslim when Ibn Umm Makhtum, the blind, asked him to recite the Quran. The blind man's insistence disrupted the conversation. The Prophet, barely concealing his anger, frowned and move on. Shortly after, a rebuke appeared in a Quranic verse: 'He frowned and turned aside when the blind man approached him'. The verse reprimanded the Prophet for paying attention to the 'disdainfully indifferent' at the cost of one who came in fear and reverence. Muhammad was chastised. A lesser man would have concealed or embroidered the episode to show himself in a better light.

For the first time in Arab society a sense of proportion, of decency, of human kindness, was institutionalized. For instance, regarding war, the Prophet's saying include: 'Looting is no more lawful than carrion', 'He has forbidden looting and mutilation' and 'He has forbidden the killing of women and children'. To pressure corrupt rulers to change their policies: 'He who commends a Sultan in what God condemns has left the religion of God'. Such sayings would in time provide a charter for action, revolution and constant renewal for Muslims. . . .

Islam Promotes Universal Humanity

Numerous points emerge from the life of the Prophet which were to have consequences both for the ideal of Islam and subsequent history. One of the main contributions of Islam was the concept of universalistic humanity transcending tribe and clan. There is no doubt that the tribe provided security to its members and a kind of stability to society. But its jealous exclusiveness based on *nasab*, ancestry, created and perpetuated divisions among people. These divisions assumed mythical proportions. Many acts of the Prophet support the claim that Islam was supreme to the tribe: his marriages outside the clan, his preference of Bilal, a black slave, as the first *muezzin* of Islam, and explicitly, for history to hear, his words at Arafat decrying race and caste divisions.

Caste, class or race would never be barriers to attaining the Muslim ideal or the highest status in Islam. A person was judged by his behaviour not his lineage—'nurture' not 'nature'. Apart from Bilal, who is something of a cult figure in Africa, many of the Muslim rulers in the Arab, Indian and Ottoman dynasties were sons of slaves. The station of 'God's viceroys on earth', the Quran's description of good human beings, is reached after *jihad*, striving and not through caste or lineage.

The Prophet was acutely aware of tribalism as it permeated his life. His support came from either his immediate kin—father's brothers, Abu Talib and Hamzah or cousins like Ali, son of

Abu Talib—or his in-laws, Abu Bakr, Umar and Uthman related by marriage. His main enemies, too, were close kin. Abu Lahab was his father's brother and Abu Suffian a relative. Within a few years of the Prophet's death, the once dominant Umayyads, who had been overshadowed by their Hashim cousins because of the Prophet, re-emerged. Muawiyah, the son of Abu Suffian, succeeded and frustrated Ali, the fourth ideal caliph. Muawiyah's dissolute son Yazid provided the gory climax to the tribal rivalry by killing Hussain, the grandson of the Prophet, just fifty years after the Prophet's death.

> *The [Muslim] ideal—with its emphasis on universal values—encouraged the building of bridges connecting groups and peoples.*

The importance of marriages in forming political alliances is illustrated in the Prophet's life. In particular, the Prophet's own marriages—once a central source of controversy for critics of Islam who wished to portray him as a debauch—are a good example of this. The importance of these marriages may be gauged from the fact that the Prophet was father-in-law to two and son-in-law to two of the four ideal caliphs. The Prophet's marriage to the daughter of Abu Suffian, one of the leading enemies of the early Muslims, helped to win him over to the cause of Islam. The Prophet's marriages also illustrate the possibility of alliances above tribalism. Some of his wives were neither kin nor of his social group. Maria the slave girl is an example. She gave birth to Ibrahim, the only male child who survived into infancy and whose death caused him unending sorrow.

An entire range of universal issues, indicating the balance between sets of opposites that maintain organized life, emerge from the Prophet's life: the struggle between the needs of *din* (religion) and *dunya* (world), between *al-akhira* (the judgment day) and *dunya*, between *dar-al-harb* and *dar-al-Islam*. These issues form the theme of Muslim history from the very beginning. The life of the Prophet balances neatly—and he constantly warned his followers on this score—*din*, religion, with *dunya*, the world. The Muslim lives in the latter by the principles of the former. He does not abandon the one for the other. He is neither blinded by the world nor rejects it to become a hermit or ascetic. Islam, the holy Quran tells us, is the middle path. It talks of the good life for human beings. In Islam the Hindu or Buddhist renunciation of the world, *dunya*, is not encouraged.

Building Bridges with Islam

Finally, the ideal—with its emphasis on universal values—encouraged the building of bridges connecting groups and peoples. In trouble the Prophet had sent Muslim groups to seek the protection of the Negus of Abyssinia. In the Kaaba when the idols were swept aside certain sources aver that he protected an icon of the virgin and child. His courtesy when receiving the Abyssinians was noted by his contemporaries. His relations with the Coptic Archbishop of Egypt were cordial (the latter sent him the white mule Duldul and Maria the slave girl). The Prophet was building bridges for Islam. His example would be followed by Muslims, culminating in the practice of the Sufi saints whose motto was *sulh-i-kul* or peace with all, and who would attract followers from all walks of life and religions.

For the Prophet the years of tribulation were brief; success followed in abundance. Within his lifetime he had established a religion and a state. Within decades of his death the banners of Islam flew on the Atlantic coast at one end of Africa, and on the banks of the river Indus in South Asia. One hundred years after his death the Islamic empire was greater than Rome at its zenith. That year [732] it was stopped at Poitiers [in France] by [seventh-century French king] Charles Martel; otherwise Europe might well have been included. Still, it stretched from the Bay of Biscay to the Indus river, from the Aral sea to the lower cataracts of the Nile. The ancient and glittering city of Damascus was the heart and capital of the empire. The world would not forgive Islam its rapid success; Muslims could not forget the memory of their early triumphs.

10

Muslims Must Denounce Violence Against Women

Irshad Manji

Irshad Manji is a journalist, television personality, and writer in residence at the University of Toronto in Canada. Born in Uganda to Muslim parents from South Asia, Manji migrated with her family to Vancouver, British Columbia, in 1972. In 2003 Manji launched a personal campaign to reform and liberalize Islam called Project Itjihad. Itjihad *refers to the Muslim tradition of adapting Islamic doctrine to new contexts. In the first phase of the project, Western women are providing financial support to Muslim women in Islamic countries to start small businesses. Manji's publications include* Rising Utopia: On the Edge of a New Democracy *(1997), and* The Trouble with Islam: A Muslim's Call for Reform in Her Faith *(2003), from which the following extract is drawn.*

Muslims must speak out against the gross human rights violations against women and minorities that characterize the Islamic world. Although some apologists for Islam claim these violations are not part of the "true Islam," many passages in the Koran teach that men have authority over women and even have the right to abuse them because men provide materially for their families. On the other hand, there are other passages in the Koran that can be interpreted as arguing for the equality of women. The Koran is full of contradictions and has been interpreted by liberals and fundamentalists to justify their own agendas. Muslims, particularly women, must recognize the Koran's imperfections and exercise their right to think for themselves.

*M*y Fellow Muslims,
    I have to be honest with you. Islam is on very thin ice with me. I'm hanging on by my fingernails, in anxiety over what's coming next from the self-appointed ambassadors of Allah [God].

When I consider all the fatwas [Islamic religious rulings] being hurled by the brain trust of our faith, I feel utter embarrassment. Don't you? I hear from a Saudi [Arabian] friend that his country's religious police arrest women for wearing red on Valentine's Day, and I think: Since when does a merciful God outlaw joy—or fun? I read about victims of rape being stoned for "adultery," and I wonder how a critical mass of us can stay stone silent.

When non-Muslims beg us to speak up, I hear you gripe that we shouldn't have to explain the behavior of other Muslims. Yet when we're misunderstood, we fail to see that it's precisely because we haven't given people a reason to think differently about us. On top of that, when I speak publicly about our failings, the very Muslims who detect stereotyping at every turn label me a sellout. A sellout to what? To moral clarity? To common decency? To civilization?

Yes, I'm blunt. You're just going to have to get used to it. In this letter, I'm asking questions from which we can no longer hide. . . . Why are we squandering the talents of women, fully half of God's creation? How can we be so sure that homosexuals deserve ostracism—or death—when the Koran states that everything God made is "excellent"? Of course, the Koran states more than that, but what's our excuse for reading the Koran literally when it's so contradictory and ambiguous?

Islamic Imperialism

Is that a heart attack you're having? Make it fast. Because if we don't speak out against the imperialists within Islam, these guys will walk away with the show. And their path leads to a dead end of more vitriol, more violence, more poverty, more exclusion. Is this the justice we seek for the world that God has leased to us? If it's not, then why don't more of us say so?

What I do hear from you is that Muslims are the targets of backlash. In France, Muslims have actually taken an author to court for calling Islam "the most stupid religion." Apparently, he's inciting hate. So we assert our rights—something most of us wouldn't have in Islamic countries. But is the French guy wrong to write that Islam needs to grow up? What about the Koran's incitement of hate against Jews? Shouldn't Muslims who invoke the Koran to justify anti-Semitism be themselves open to a lawsuit? Or would this amount to more "backlash"? What makes us righteous and everybody else racist?

> *We've got to end Islam's totalitarianism, particularly the gross human rights violations against women and religious minorities.*

Through our screaming self-pity and our conspicuous silences, we Muslims are conspiring against ourselves. We're in crisis, and we're dragging the rest of the world with us. If ever there was a moment for an Islamic reformation, it's now. For the love of God, what are we doing about it?

Ending Islamic Totalitarianism

You may wonder who I am to talk to you this way. I am a Muslim Refusenik. That doesn't mean I refuse to be a Muslim; it simply means I refuse to join an army of automatons in the name of Allah. I take this phrase from the original refuseniks—Soviet Jews who championed religious and personal freedom. Their communist masters refused to let them emigrate to Israel. For their attempts to leave the Soviet Union, many refuseniks paid with hard labor and, sometimes, with their lives. Over time, though, their persistent refusal to comply with the mechanisms of mind control and soullessness helped end a totalitarian system.

Not solely because of September 11, but more urgently because of it, we've got to end Islam's totalitarianism, particularly the gross human rights violations against women and religious minorities. You'll want to assure me that what I'm describing in this open letter to you isn't "true" Islam. Frankly, such a distinction wouldn't have impressed Prophet Muhammad, who said that religion is the way we conduct ourselves toward others—not theoretically, but actually. By that standard, how Muslims behave *is* Islam. To sweep that reality under the rug is to absolve ourselves of responsibility for our fellow human beings. See why I'm struggling?

As I view it, the trouble with Islam is that lives are small and lies are big. Totalitarian impulses lurk in mainstream Islam. That's one hell of a charge, I know. Please hear me out. I'll show you what I mean, as calmly as I possibly can. . . .

Growing Up in a Muslim Household

At home, my father's ready fist ensured his family's obedience to an arbitrary domestic drill. *Don't laugh at dinner. When I steal your savings, shut up. When I kick your ass, remember, it'll be harder next time. When I pound your mother, don't call the police. If they show up, I'll charm them into leaving, and you know they will. The moment they're gone, I'll slice off your ear. If you threaten to alert social services, I'll amputate your other ear.*

> *Unremitting subservience would have been my lot if we'd stayed in the confines of Muslim Uganda.*

The one time my father chased me through the house with a knife, I managed to fly out of my bedroom window and spend the night on the roof. My mum had no idea of my situation because she was working the graveyard shift at an airline company. Just as well; I'm not sure I would have crawled down for any promise of safety she might have offered. For the same reason that I liked my school [in Richmond, Vancouver] and Rose of Sharon Baptist Church [where Manji took Sunday School lessons as a small child in Richmond] and, years later, Aberdeen Centre [also in Richmond], I liked the roof. From each of these perches, I could survey a world of open-ended possibility. In the East African Muslim community from which I came, would I have been allowed to dream of a formal education? Of landing scholarships? Of participating in political races, never mind holding office? To judge by the grainy black-and-white photos that showed me, at age three, playing a bride with her head covered, hands folded, eyes downcast, and legs dangling from the sofa, I can only guess that unremitting subservience would have been my lot if we'd stayed in the confines of Muslim Uganda. How's that for a firm grasp of the obvious?

> *The woman, her dignity already violated . . . still faced 180 lashes! How . . . could I reconcile such an elemental injustice with my Muslim faith?*

The bigger question is this: Why did the Richmond madressa [Islamic school in Vancouver, Canada], set up by immigrants to this land of rights and freedoms, choose autocracy? From age nine to age fourteen, I spent every Saturday there. Classes took place on the upper floor of the newly built mosque, which resembled a mammoth suburban house more than it did Middle Eastern architecture. Inside, however, you got stern Islam through and through. Men and women entered the mosque by different doors and planted themselves on the correct sides of an immovable wall that cut the building in half, quarantining the sexes during worship. Set in this wall was a door that connected the men's and women's sides. This came in handy after services, when men would demand more food from the communal kitchen by thrusting their bowls through the door, banging on the wall, and waiting mere seconds for a woman's arm to thrust back the replenished bowls. In the mosque, men never had to see women, and women never had to be seen. If that isn't the definition of assigning us small lives, then I'm missing something big.

No Dignity for Women at the Madressa

One flight up was the madressa, with its depressing decor of burnt-brown rugs, fluorescent lights, and portable partitions that separated the girls from the boys. Wherever classes congregated within the wide expanse of that room, a partition would tag along. Worse was the partition between mind and soul. In my Saturday classes I learned that if you're spiritual, you don't think. If you think, you're not spiritual. This facile equation rubbed up against the exhilarating curiosity in me that Richmond indulged. Call it my personal clash of civilizations.

The solution wasn't simply to accept that there's a secular

world and a nonsecular one, and that each has its ways of being. By that logic, the decidedly nonsecular Rose of Sharon Baptist Church should have quashed my questions. Instead, my curiosity brought me praise there. At Burnett Junior High, a secular school, my questions bugged the bejeezus out of my vice-principal but nobody shut me down. In both places, the dignity of the individual prevailed. Not so at my madressa. I entered its premises wearing a white polyester chador [Muslim head covering] and departed several hours later with my hair flattened and my spirit deflated, as if the condom over my head had properly inoculated me from "unsafe" intellectual activity. . . .

Koran Provides No Answers

The trouble began with *Know Your Islam*, the primer that I packed in my madressa bag every week. After reading it, I needed to know more about "my" Islam. Why must girls observe the essentials, such as praying five times a day, at an earlier age than boys? Because, [my madressa teacher] Mr. Khaki told me, girls mature sooner. They reach the "obligatory age" of practice at nine compared to thirteen for boys.

"Then why not reward girls for our maturity by letting us lead prayer?" I asked.

"Girls can't lead prayer."

"What do you mean?"

"Girls aren't permitted."

"Why not?"

"Allah says so."

"What's His reason?"

"Read the Koran."

> *The Koran is not transparently egalitarian for women. It's not transparently anything except enigmatic.*

I tried, though it felt artificial since I didn't know Arabic. Do I see you nodding your head? Most Muslims have no clue what we're saying when we're reciting the Koran in Arabic. It's not that we're obtuse. Rather, Arabic is one of the world's most rhythmic languages, and weekly lessons at the madressa simply don't let us grasp its intricacies. *Haram*, for instance, can refer to something forbidden or something sacred, depending on which "a" you stress. Forbidden versus sacred: We're not talking subtle shifts in meaning here. To the inherent challenges of this language, add the realities of life. In my case, a violent father who practiced religion mostly for show and a mother who did her best to be devout while striving to sustain a household on shift work. You can appreciate why Arabic study failed to rate as a family priority. Frankly, Mr. Khaki's stock reply to my questions—"Read the Koran"—fell about as flat as my chador-chastened hair. . . .

> *The Koran is so profoundly at war with itself that Muslims who 'live by the book' have no choice but to choose what to emphasize and what to downplay.*

What did I learn about why girls can't lead prayer? I can't tell you right now. Because even if mullahs [Islamic religious scholars] and madressa teachers supply pat answers, the Koran doesn't. What I can tell you is that in between elections, drama rehearsals, part-time jobs, volleyball practices—up to, into, and beyond university—I made my way through the scripture with the "woman question" top of mind. I'm still reading. To divulge my conclusions . . . would be to leapfrog into my adult life. . . .

Questions About Islam

My career as a TV journalist and commentator placed me on the front line of the public's own questions about Islam. . . .

Two questions, in particular, have rocked my world—both for the better, but neither without pain.

The first question is, "How do you reconcile homosexuality with Islam?" I'm openly lesbian. I choose to be "out" because, having matured in a miserable household under a father who despised joy, I'm not about to sabotage the consensual love that offers me joy as an adult. I met my first girlfriend in my twenties and, weeks afterwards, told my mother about the relationship. She responded like the wonderful parent she is. So the question of whether I could be a Muslim and a lesbian at the same time barely unsettled me. *That* was religion. *This* was happiness. I knew which one I needed more. I carried on, intermittently studying Islam, learning the fine art of sustaining relationships with women (which is another book unto itself), producing television programs, and generally living the multidirectional life of a twenty-something in North America. . . .

Injustice in Islam

Now for the second question I promised to tell you about. It was asked of me mere months before September 11, and it precipitated my biggest test of faith.

> **//***Reform isn't about telling ordinary Muslims what not to think, but about giving Islam's 1 billion devotees permission to think.***//**

In December 2000, an interoffice envelope arrived on my desk at *QueerTelevision*.[1] The envelope came from my boss, Moses Znaimer. Scrambling to complete as many episodes of the program as possible by Christmas break, I felt at once drained and in need of distraction. So I opened the envelope and pulled out a newspaper clipping. It featured a brief report from the [French press agency] *Agence France-Presse:*

GIRL COERCED INTO SEX TO RECEIVE 180 LASHES

Tsafe [Nigeria]. A pregnant 17-year-old whom an Islamic court sentenced to 180 lashes for premarital sex will give birth within days, her family said yesterday.

Bariya Ibrahim Magazu told the court in September that she had been pushed into having sex with three men who were associates of her father. The girl produced seven witnesses. The girl's family said she was due to give birth within a couple of days and was expected to receive her punishment at least 40 days later.

1. In 1998 Manji hosted programs for Canada's *QueerTelevision*, a station catering to the interests of homosexuals.

In vibrant red ink, Moses had circled the word "Islamic," twice underlined the number "180," and penned a comment, Talmud-style [truncated style from Jewish legal interpretations], in the margins. It read:

> IRSHAD
> ONE OF THESE
> DAYS YOU'LL
> TELL ME HOW
> YOU RECONCILE
> THIS KIND OF
> INSANITY,
> AND FEMALE
> GENITAL
> MUTILATION,
> WITH YOUR
> MUSLIM
> FAITH.
> M.

Oy vey. Wasn't it enough that viewers of *QueerTelevision* goaded me to choose between my sexual orientation and my spiritual orientation? Did my boss have to burden me ethically, too? Especially at a time of excruciating deadlines?

I pushed the envelope aside and got on with working for the man. But over the next several hours, Moses's challenge shook my conscience. Tell me it doesn't do the same to yours. The story of this young rape victim has to haunt any decent human being because, whatever the minutiae of her case, one reported fact couldn't be rationalized away: The woman, her dignity already violated, had gone to the trouble of rounding up seven witnesses. Seven! And she still faced 180 lashes! How the hell could I reconcile such an elemental injustice with my Muslim faith?

I was going to have to address it head-on. Not with defensiveness, not with theories, but with total honesty. . . .

The Koran on Women

I felt ready not only to confront Moses's challenge, but to expand on it. . . . What does the Koran say? . . . Does it unequivocally, or even plausibly, support whipping a raped woman despite a multitude of witnesses to the crime against her? While we're at it, does the Koran really prohibit women from leading prayer?

For the next few months, I reread Islam's holy book with eyes open wider and defenses further down than at any other point in my life.

In the beginning, there was the woman question. Whom did God create first—Adam or Eve? The Koran is dead silent on this distinction. God breathed life into a "single soul," and from that soul he "created its spouse." Who's the soul and who's the spouse? It's irrelevant.

> *The Koran is a bundle of contradictions, at least when it comes to women.*

Moreover, there's no mention of Adam's rib, from which, according to the Bible, Eve was made. Nor does the Koran suggest Adam to taste forbidden fruit. Bottom line: You can't find fodder here for male superiority. Just the opposite, in fact. The Koran cautions Muslims to remember that they're not God, so men and women had better be fair in demanding their rights from one another. And topping off this passage is a seemingly female-friendly flourish: "Honor the mothers who bore you. God is ever watching over you."

Strange thing is, in the same chapter—mere lines away—the Koran completely reverses course. It says: "Men have authority over women because God has made the one superior to the other, and because they spend their wealth to maintain them. Good women are obedient. . . . As for those from whom you fear disobedience, admonish them, forsake them in beds apart, and beat them."

Contradictions in the Koran

Let me get this straight: To deserve a beating, a woman doesn't actually have to disobey anybody, a man merely has to fear her disobedience. His insecurity becomes her problem. Swell. I know I'm oversimplifying, but oversimplification runs rampant in the development of god-awful laws. I'll give you a concrete example. One line from the Koran—that men can lord it over women because they "spend their wealth to maintain" them—has influenced the Cairo Declaration, the specious human rights charter endorsed by Muslim countries in 1990.

Sure, one clause of the charter affirms that women and men en-joy equal dignity. But the next clause designates men as the providers of their families. It's not expressing a *preference* for men as providers, it's making an outright proclamation that "the husband is responsible for the support and welfare of the family." And since the Koran states that husbands can claim "authority over women" through the role of providing, you fig-ure out the rest.

In light of the raped woman in Nigeria, one more passage from the Koran bowled me over. "Women are your fields," it says. "Go, then, into your fields when you please. Do good works and fear God." Huh? Go into women when you please, yet do good? Are women partners or property? Partners, insists Jamal Badawi, a renowned Koranic scholar. He assures me that this "sexually enlightened" verse serves as a defense of foreplay. Like fields, women need tender loving care in order to turn sperm into real human beings. The farmer's "seed is worthless unless you have the fertile land that will give it growth," Badawi says, looking quite satisfied with his progressive explanation. But he has only addressed the words, "Go into your fields." What about the words, "when you please"? Doesn't that quali-fier give men undue power? The question remains: Which par-adigm does Allah advocate—Adam and Eve as equals, or women as land to be plowed (excuse me, stroked) on a whim?

The truth is, I knew which interpretation I wanted but I didn't know for sure (and still don't) which one God wanted. With so much contradiction at play, nobody knows. Those who wish to flog women on the flimsiest of charges can get the necessary backup from the Koran. So can those who don't want girls to lead prayer. Then again, those who seek equality can find succor, too.

The Koran Is at War with Itself

In trying to answer how I reconcile my Muslim faith with the barbaric lashing of a rape victim, I concluded that I couldn't rec-oncile them with breezy confidence. I couldn't glibly say, as I've heard so many Muslim feminists do, that the Koran itself guar-antees justice. I couldn't cavalierly shrug that those whacko Nigerian jurists who apply Sharia law have sodomized my trans-parently egalitarian religion. The Koran is not transparently egalitarian for women. It's not transparently anything except enigmatic. With apologies to [American political commentator]

Noam Chomsky, it's Muslims who manufacture consent in Allah's name. The decisions we make on the basis of the Koran aren't dictated by God; we make them of our free human will.

Sounds obvious to a mainstream Christian or Jew, but it's not obvious to a Muslim who's been raised to believe—as most of us have—that the Koran lays it all out for us in a "straight path," and that our sole duty, and right, is to imitate it. This is a big lie. Do you hear me? A big, beard-faced lie.

Far from being perfect, the Koran is so profoundly at war with itself that Muslims who "live by the book" have no choice but to choose what to emphasize and what to downplay. Maybe that's the easy part—any one of us can rationalize our biases by elevating one verse and ignoring another. Which, by the way, liberals do as much as militants, airbrushing the negative noise of the Koran at least as much as our opponents expunge its positive pronouncements. We all have agendas, some more equal than others.

But as long as we're caught up in this endgame of proving that "our" dogma trumps "their" dogma, we're losing sight of the greater challenge. That is, to openly question the perfection of the Koran so that the stampede to reach a correct conclusion about what it "really" says will slow down and, over time, become an exercise in literacy instead of literalism. At this stage, reform isn't about telling ordinary Muslims what not to think, but about giving Islam's 1 billion devotees permission to think. Since the Koran is a bundle of contradictions, at least when it comes to women, we have every reason to think.

11

Muslim Women Have More Rights, Respect, and Protection than Western Women

Afsar Bano

Indian scholar Afsar Bano has written several books on Eastern women's lives, including Indian Women: The Changing Face *(2003) and* Women and Social Change *(2003).*

When Islam was founded in the seventh century, women in the East were freed from oppression and injustice and given their due rights. Women in the West, on the other hand, were denied these rights until the modern age when the idea of the equality of the sexes was advanced through the women's liberation movement. Although this movement has bestowed some benefits on Western women, it has also overburdened them with political and economic roles in addition to their traditional roles as wives and mothers. As a result, the institution of the family has broken down in the West. In addition, Western women have not succeeded in obtaining equal rights with men. In contrast, under Islamic law, women's rights have been protected and the sanctity of the family has been safeguarded. Islam holds out the promise of liberating humanity from the deplorable social conditions that characterize the modern world.

Afsar Bano, *Status of Women in Islamic Society, Volume II—Family*. New Dehli, India: Anmol Publications PVT. LTD., 2003. Copyright © 2003 by Afsar Bano. Reproduced by permission.

D uring the course of history woman has long been the oppressed section of the society. She had been exploited in
Greece, Rome (Byzantine empire), Egypt, Iraq, India, China
and Arabia. She was sold and purchased in market places and
fairs and was treated worse than animals. For a long time a debate continued on the issue whether the woman had a soul.
The Arabs regarded her very existence as a disgrace, and some
cruel and totally insensitive persons used to bury their daugh-
ters alive at or soon after birth. In India the widow was consigned to flames at the funeral pyre of her dead husband. The
religious faiths given to asceticism regarded her as the source of
sin, the door leading to transgression and contact with her was
considered an impediment in spiritual development and salvation. In most civilizations of the world she enjoyed no place in
society. She was contemptible and despised in their estimate.
She had no social and political rights. She could not exercise
her own free will in any financial deal. She was under the tute-
lage of her father, later under the oppressive rule of the tyrant
of a husband and lastly under the patronising care of the male
offspring. She was not permitted by long standing conventions
to challenge their authority and she had no course of justice to
appeal to by way of escape from tyranny and excesses—not
even a breath of complaint.

Undoubtedly she has at times been in the seat of authority
in some parts of the world. And it is also on record in the world
history that empires and governments have danced to her
tune, even tantrums, and it has been a common occurrence
that she has had ascendancy in familial, tribal and monarchial
activities. In some uncivilized tribes she had enjoyed superiority and rule and there are remnants of it still to be seen. Yet as
female of the human species, there was little change in her status and she suffered in silence through the course of history
and remained deprived of her due rights as usual.

Islam Rescued Women

Islam took her out of this whirlpool of oppression and tyranny,
meted out justice to her, granting her due rights, elevating her
position in honour and dignity and teaching the society to respect her. But the Western nations that failed to come under the
benign shade of Islam remained deprived of its blessings and
healthy effects. In their societies woman's rights and privileges
remained trodden under the feet of the dominant sex and she,

poor thing, did put up with all that uncomplaining. In the modern age (even long after Renaissance) the reaction and changes in the social fabric of the society and the concept of the equality of the sexes came to the fore, arguments were put forth in support of this claim and attempts were made to prove that in spite of differences between the sexes woman was not inferior to man. Both stand on an equal footing in all respects and this position does not permit of any discrimination whatsoever. She can do everything that a man is capable of, and can hold any office of responsibility placed under her charge. She is free from all shackles and restrictions and man's ascendancy over her must cease, and as such she must enjoy all the rights and privileges that have formerly been the monopoly of the stronger sex.

> **" Islam took her out of this whirlpool of oppression . . . , meted out justice to her, granting her due rights, elevating her position in honour and dignity. "**

It was a very pleasing and flattering concept for the woman, and she picked up this offer of the society and appeared to have regained her lost dignity. Gradually she became the partner of man on equal terms in economic, social and cultural affairs. Soon she was found striving in factories, offices and colleges, shoulder to shoulder with her male counterpart, nay, taking part freely in the outdoor activities in parks, clubs, picnic spots as well as in domestic circles with men. Her presence was considered essential in every walk of life and without her, life appeared colourless and drab. The female sex considered it a step towards her progress and exaltation and appeared impatiently eager to take one step after another on the road to success and elation. She was dazzled by its apparent lustre but failed to see through its hidden evils and detriment.

Harmful Effects of Woman's Liberation

The concept of woman's lib put forth by the West was beneficial to her in some respects but harmful as adjudged from other angles. If she had been emancipated from the tyranny of man on the one side, no allowance had been made for her physical faculties, capabilities, temperament and psychological make-up in this (man's) 'benevolence' to her. This change had come as a strong reaction against man's tyranny and injustice to the weaker sex and had, hidden in it, all those sources of intemperance and excesses that are usually met with in such violent, uncontrolled reactions.

This unbridled freedom of woman has given the entire life-pattern of the West a dangerously faulty orientation and has created conditions of imbalance giving rise to terrible consequences. At this juncture Islam comes to our aid and guidance in the right direction. It gives assurance of the fundamental rights of woman and her all-round progress and development as well as provides safeguards against the devastating and disgraceful consequences with which the West is faced at present. Some of the social and political consequences are briefly mentioned here.

Decadence of Western Civilization

As a result of free mixing of sexes, with temerity, in every sphere of life, the trend of profligacy and dissoluteness came into existence and developed. And adultery and fornication became rife. And this gave rise to a shameless and disgraceful culture which ultimately left no room for morality and shocked the sense of modesty and noblemindedness, both being strangulated and done away with.

> *This unbridled freedom of woman has given the entire life-pattern of the West a dangerously faulty orientation.*

History bears testimony to the fact that whenever the woman was dragged out of her citadel, her home, as the centre of attraction in social functions and other public gatherings, it created conditions for unrestrained dissipation of excited passions, and the stink of moral turpitude, normally unbearable even behind the closed doors was now out in the open, vitiating the healthy atmosphere. Even the most sacred and strictly prohibited relations were no more sacred and inviolable, and were being desecrated with impunity. Not to say of ordinary mortals, their gods and goddesses were implicated and their images tarnished, presenting them as emblems of debauchery. Such shameful and ignoble conduct was ascribed to them that it mortified their own humble devotees. Prostitutes and other women of ill-repute attained that exalted position in their corrupt society which their chaste and modest counterparts in their homes had never contemplated. Art and culture came to the aid of degenerate sex and unrestrained passions and beautifully explained them away as the most natural phenomenon of the human nature. Female charms were brought to the public view through paintings and photographs in the nude, and the sculptors fashioned stark naked statues leaving no details of the charms of the female figure in their zeal of promoting their own erotic art. Even goddesses were not spared by their degenerate sex-ridden art. Man revelled in the charms of the female form, leaving nothing for imagination, and her no less enchanting voice was exploited to attract them towards promiscuity, immodesty and sin. Fiction, drama, poetry and literature in various other forms depicted sex in all its lurid forms and shameful details and the accompanying sensations and passions. Women had become toys in the hands of man to play with as they were pleased and as much as they liked. She finally came to mean to him an outlet for the dissipation of overwrought passions in an atmosphere surcharged with eroticism. Culture and civilization became an ignoble record of sex activities and its manifold manifestations so that they seemed to revolve round them alone. The evil effects of unbridled sex brought the one time mighty cultures and civilizations to decadence, decay and annihilation. Rome (the Byzantine empire as called by the Arabs), Egypt, Persia and Babylonia followed the same path of decline and death, their one-time glory and pomp of power not withstanding. Our modern civilization too, is rushing headlong at a dangerous pace to the same sad end. Probably the time is not far off when the apparently mighty and glorious edifice will collapse tottering down and crumble to dust (without any [Edward] Gibbon [eighteenth-century British historian, author of *The Decline and Fall of the Roman Empire*] to lament its fall). And from its ashes a more healthy culture would emerge.

Decline of the Family

The familial order remained intact due to the presence of a woman to manage its affairs internally. But when and where her activities found fields in the world outside and her time got occupied mostly by them, the familial system broke down. Whatever she gained in the world outside, she had to pay dearly for it in the form of destruction of her home. Family is the foundation-stone of society and when it got displaced the entire edifice became topsy turvy. Woman was an angel of mercy, a source of comfort and solace to man, but now no more. The deep rooted conjugal relationship of love that bound them together to face the ups and downs of life was gone, creating a vacuum, and each one was left alone to fend for himself/herself. The relationship of the parents and the offspring became weakened gradually. The parents are the centre of affection and love for the children. It was no more their privilege, and (as useless members of society and the families) they were consigned to the nursing homes. The offspring is the sole support of the parents in their old age. Gone was this support for them to lean on, and they were compelled by the changed circumstances and estranged relationships to pass their last days in poor houses or old age asylums, forlorn and broken-hearted. And it did not end there. All other relationships that depended on the survival of of the family also disappeared with it. And man became woefully deprived of peace and blessings only the family circle can provide. Breaking down of the family is no small issue. It is such a heavy loss that no society can put up with it for long. Finally this breaking down of the family ruins the society also. No edifice can exist without a foundation.

Islam and the Family

Islam regards a well-knit family essential for the survival of the society, since it rests on that foundation alone. The strength and firmness of the family is the firmness of the society and vice versa. Islam provides very strong and firm foundations for the family and guards it against those factors that would weaken its fabric or be its undoing. It has established an entire system for it and furnished detailed information with certain limits and regulations as necessary safeguards. It lays great stress on keeping this system and organisation intact and that the limits prescribed by Allah be vigilantly guarded against their violation. In this set-up woman has prime importance. She plays an important role in its smooth and regular functioning. She has her rights and privileges as well as her obligations in it. If she were to detach herself from this organisation and fail to meet her responsibilities, not just squarely but devotedly, it will collapse before long. It can last only as long as the woman in the structure keeps striving hard for its maintenance and her attention remains centred on it alone.

Injustice to Women

A disproportion was noticed in the rights and obligations of woman and the usual balance and moderation (guaranteeing proper functioning of a happy home) departed. Nature brings up and develops her to take upon herself the onerous burden of becoming a mother, so that the human species may be nursed and brought up in her loving lap. The passions and feelings, powers and capabilities called for in this difficult job of great care and responsibility have also been provided to her by nature. That is why she has an inborn strong motive to meet this natural demand. Becoming a mother and promoting a human generation is not a casual and momentary pastime but a long drawn and painstaking job, having its toilsome periods like pregnancy, delivery, breast-feeding, upbringing of the child and its education and training. In this tiring function of hers, man gives her a helping hand in some phases and also cooperates with her, indirectly though, but directly he can neither bear her burden nor does he do so in practical life. The burden has to be borne by woman alone, which takes the greater part of her energies and capabilities. Now, if she is burdened with all those political, social and economic responsibilities also which is entirely man's spheres of activity, over and above those of running a household and managing the family affairs, it would be an excess and great injustice. It may become justifiable only in case she is relieved of the burden which nature has imposed on her, and developed her accordingly in a peculiar manner. But so long as a woman remains a woman, and her pure and unsullied sentiments and her best capabilities are in demand for the survival of the human race through offspring, its growth and development and upbringing, this burden shall be too much for her to bear. It can neither be taken away from her through any artifice nor a proper substitute can be found for it.

Islam Offers a Better Life

On this count Islam presents a moderate and well-balanced view as a solution of the problem. It confers on woman all those economic, political and social rights which are granted to man. However, she has been kept out of certain responsibilities which are alien to her temperament and her physical build, as also the additional burden with which she cannot squarely meet her natural responsibilities. An example may be helpful in the comprehension of the issue under discussion. The head of an Islamic state can only be male and the defence of the country is the business of men only. Although she has not been burdened with these exclusively male responsibilities, she enjoys all other political rights. She can express her opinion in politics or offer suggestions on political issues. She has the right of criticism and reckoning (calling to account). She can point out the mistake of any office-bearer, even the head of the Islamic state publicly. No checks or bars can be put on this right of hers. Let us take another example. She has no economic responsibilities but has the right to undertake economic enterprises within the limits prescribed by Islam.

> *The evil effects of unbridled sex brought the one time mighty cultures . . . to decadence, decay and annihilation.*

Owing to the heavy responsibilities imposed by Islam on man it has also conferred on him more rights to enable him to meet them easily. But perfect justice has been kept in view here too, and it has been given due regard that this does not spell injustice to woman. For this purpose Islam has put very stringent checks on man so that safety of woman's rights becomes a certainty. In the family, man is the custodian and guardian. But this position does not give him a free hand to curtail woman's rights and privileges or be guilty of excesses in any other form. Whenever he oversteps his limits of authority there is the Islamic law to hold his hand and punish him if necessary. Even the head of the state has no right to lay his hand upon her life, property, honour and dignity and her other individual and collective rights. For any breach of law in this regard, he will be called to account like any other citizen of the land.

As the last word it has to be admitted that man has undoubtedly been guilty of great excesses in his dealings with woman. But there is also in him a natural passion of sympathy and love for her. Islam also stirs up that passion in him and develops it, induces him to not only meet his obligations to her for fulfilment of her rights, but to be had sympathetic to her with benevolence in his attitude, for she deserves it. This passion has a fundamental importance in this mutual relationship of man and wife. In the present age the struggle for rights between man and woman has harmed this passion and it is half-dead. At times it appears that the passion is dead. To the woman it has been a great loss. For, law alone, however perfect in its effectiveness and impressed upon men's minds with great force, cannot solve the problems. That is why notwithstanding persistent claims of equality between man and woman, it is nowhere visible in practical life of even its zealous protagonists. She does not fully enjoy the social rights conferred on her by law and in certain situations, she is at the last limit of suffering tyranny and excesses. She is a market commodity sold and purchased to gratify the lust of man. She is being invaded and her life and property and honour and dignity are in great peril. Her chastity and modesty too are at stake being plundered unhesitatingly. It appears it is becoming increasingly difficult for her to defend herself from the everyday changing pattern of attacks on her at every step.

The bare fact is that even if certain rights are recognized for a weak party, it is not easy for it to have them honoured. Woman cannot wrest from man the rights in her fight for them. She can succeed only in case the man is willing to allow them to her. Towards that sympathy for her and love of man are essential, whereby he may come to regard oppression and tyranny to her a serious crime, a heinous sin. Islam has achieved unparalleled success in this behalf. And whenever this experiment in the history of mankind shall be repeated, human society shall once again witness the beautiful spring after a dismal and devastating autumn, as the world witnessed it earlier in the midst of deplorable conditionings similar to our own or even worse.

Organizations to Contact

The editors have compiled the following list of organizations concerned with the issues debated in this book. The descriptions are derived from materials provided by the organizations. All the organizations have publications or information available for interested readers. The list was compiled on the date of publication of the present volume; names, addresses, and phone numbers may change. Be aware that many organizations take several weeks or longer to respond to inquiries, so allow as much time as possible.

American-Arab Anti-Discrimination Committee (ADC)
4201 Connecticut Ave. NW, Suite 300, Washington, DC 20008
(202) 244-2990 • fax: (202) 244-3196
e-mail: ADC@adc.org • Web site: www.adc.org

This organization fights anti-Arab stereotyping in the media and discrimination and hate crimes against Arab Americans. It publishes a bimonthly newsletter, the *Chronicle;* issue papers and special reports; community studies; legal, media, and educational guides; and action alerts.

AMIDEAST
1730 M St. NW, Suite 1100, Washington, DC 20036-4505
(202) 776-9600 • fax: (202) 776-7000
e-mail: inquiries@amideast.org • Web site: www.amideast.org

AMIDEAST promotes understanding and cooperation between Americans and the people of the Middle East and North Africa through education and development programs. It publishes a number of books for all age groups, including *Islam: A Primer.*

Arab World and Islamic Resources (AWAIR)
2137 Rose St., Berkeley, CA 94709
(510) 704-0517
e-mail: awair@igc.org • Web site: www.awaironline.org

AWAIR provides materials and services for educators teaching about the Arab world and about Islam at the precollege level. It publishes books and videos, including the *Arab World Studies Notebook, Middle Eastern Muslim Women Speak,* and *Muhammad: His Life Based on the Earliest Sources.*

Canadian Islamic Congress (CIC)
420 Erb St. West, Suite 424, Waterloo, ON N2L 6K6 Canada
(519) 746-1242 • fax: (519) 746-2929
Web site: www.cicnow.com

CIC's stated goals are to establish a national Canadian network of Muslim individuals and organizations; to act in matters affecting the rights and welfare of Canadian Muslims; and to present the interests of Canadian Muslims to Canadian governments, political parties, media, and other organizations. Its publications include research reports examining the coverage of Islam in the Canadian media and articles including "Jihad: Waging Peace and Justice."

Council on American-Islamic Relations (CAIR)
453 New Jersey Ave. SE, Washington, DC 20003
(202) 488-8787 • fax: (202) 488-0833
e-mail: cair@cair-net.org • Web site: www.cair-net.org

CAIR is a nonprofit membership organization that presents an Islamic perspective to public policy issues and challenges misrepresentations of Islam and Muslims. It fights discrimination against Muslims in America and lobbies political leaders on issues related to Islam. Its publications include the quarterly newsletter *CAIR News*, reports on Muslim civil rights issues, and periodic action alerts.

International Institute of Islamic Thought
500 Grove St., Herndon, VA 20170-4735
(703) 471-1133 • fax: (703) 471-3922
e-mail: iiit@iiit.org • Web site: www.iiit.org

This nonprofit academic research facility promotes and coordinates research and related activities in Islamic philosophy, the humanities, and social sciences. It publishes numerous books in both Arabic and English as well as the quarterly *American Journal of Islamic Social Science* and the *Muslim World Book Review*.

Islamic Circle of North America (ICNA)
166-26 Eighty-ninth Ave., Jamaica, NY 11432
(718) 658-1199 • fax: (718) 658-1255
e-mail: info@icna.org • Web site: www.icna.org

ICNA works to propagate Islam as a way of life and to establish an Islamic system in North America. It maintains a charitable relief organization and publishes numerous pamphlets in its Islamic Da'wah series as well as the monthly magazine *Message*.

Islamic Information Center of America (IICA)
PO Box 4052, Des Plaines, IL 60016
(847) 541-8141 • fax: (847) 824-8436
e-mail: president@iica.org • Web site: www.iica.org

IICA is a nonprofit organization that provides information about Islam to Muslims, the general public, and the media. It publishes and distributes a number of pamphlets and a monthly newsletter, the *Invitation*.

Islamic Supreme Council of America (ISCA)
17195 Silver Pkwy., #401, Fenton, MI 48430
(810) 593-1222 • fax: (810) 815-0518
e-mail: staff@islamicsupremecouncil.org
Web site: www.islamicsupremecouncil.org

ISCA is a nongovernmental religious organization that promotes Islam in America both by providing practical solutions to American Muslims in integrating Islamic teachings with American culture and by teaching non-Muslims that Islam is a religion of moderation, peace, and tolerance. It strongly condemns Islamic extremists and all forms of terrorism. Its Web site includes statements, commentaries, and reports on terrorism, including *Usama bin Laden: A Legend Gone Wrong, The Honor of Women in Islam*, and *Jihad: A Misunderstood Concept from Islam*.

Islamic Texts Society
22A Brooklands Ave., Cambridge, UK CB2 2DQ
USA (800) 944-6190
e-mail: info@its.org.uk • Web site: www.its.org.uk

This organization aims to promote a greater understanding of Islam and publishes and sells English translations of works of importance to the faith and culture of Muslims. Among the titles it offers is *Ideals and Realities of Islam* and *Unveiling Islam*.

Middle East Institute
1761 N St. NW, Washington, DC 20036-2882
(202) 785-1141 • fax: (202) 331-8861
e-mail: mideasti@mideast.org
Web site: www.themiddleeastinstitute.org

The institute's charter mission is to promote better understanding of Middle Eastern cultures, languages, religions, and politics. It publishes numerous books, papers, audiotapes, and videos as well as the quarterly *Middle East Journal*. It also maintains an educational outreach department to give teachers and students of all grade levels advice on resources.

Middle East Media Research Institute (MEMRI)
PO Box 27837, Washington, DC 20038-7837
(202) 955-9070 • fax: (202) 955-9077
e-mail: memri@memri.org • Web site: www.memri.org

MEMRI translates and disseminates articles and commentaries from Middle East media sources and provides original research and analysis on the region. Its Jihad and Terrorism Studies Project monitors radical Islamic groups and individuals and their reactions to acts of terrorism around the world.

Middle East Studies Association
University of Arizona, 1219 N. Santa Rita Ave., Tucson, AZ 85721
(520) 621-5850 • fax: (520) 626-9095
e-mail: mesana@u.arizona.edu
Web site: http://w3fp.arizona.edu/mesassoc

This professional academic association of scholars on the Middle East focuses particularly on the rise of Islam. It publishes the quarterly *International Journal of Middle East Studies* and runs a project for the evaluation of textbooks for coverage of the Middle East.

Muslim Public Affairs Council (MPAC)
3010 Wilshire Blvd., Suite 217, Los Angeles, CA 90010
(213) 383-3443 • fax: (213) 383-9674
e-mail: salam@mpac.org • Web site: www.mpac.org

MPAC is a nonprofit public service agency that strives to disseminate accurate information about Muslims and achieve cooperation between various communities on the basis of shared values such as peace, justice, freedom, and dignity. It publishes and distributes the *Minaret Magazine* and a number of reports on issues of concern to the Muslim community, such as U.S. foreign relations and human rights policy.

Washington Institute for Near East Policy
1828 L St. NW, Suite 1050, Washington, DC 20036
(202) 452-0650 • fax: (202) 223-5364
e-mail: info@washingtoninstitute.org
Web site: www.washingtoninstitute.org

The institute is an independent, nonprofit research organization that provides information and analysis on the Middle East and U.S. policy in the region. It publishes numerous books, periodic monographs, and reports on regional politics, security, and economics, including *Fight on All Fronts: Hizballah, the War on Terror, and the War in Iraq* and *Targeting Terror: U.S. Policy Toward Middle Eastern State Sponsors and Terrorist Organizations, Post–September 11.*

Bibliography

Books

Mohammad Abu-Nimar	*Nonviolence and Peace in Islam: Theory and Practice.* Gainesville: University Press of Florida, 2003.
Akbar S. Ahmed	*Islam Under Siege: Living Dangerously in a Post-Honor World.* Cambridge, UK: Polity, 2003.
M.J. Akbar	*The Shade of Swords: Jihad and the Conflict Between Islam and Christianity.* London: Routledge, 2002.
Tariq Ali	*The Clash of Fundamentalisms: Crusades, Jihads, and Modernity.* New York: Verso, 2002.
Karen Armstrong	*Islam: A Short History.* New York: Random House, 2000.
John L. Esposito, ed.	*The Oxford Dictionary of Islam.* New York: Oxford University Press, 2003.
John L. Esposito, ed.	*Unholy War: Terror in the Name of Islam.* Oxford: Oxford University Press, 2002.
John L. Esposito, ed.	*What Everyone Needs to Know About Islam.* New York: Oxford University Press, 2002.
Reuven Firestone	*Jihad: The Origin of Holy War in Islam.* New York: Oxford University Press, 1999.
Fred Halliday	*Islam and the Myth of Confrontation: Religion and Politics in the Middle East.* New York: I.B. Tauris, 2003.
Asma Gull Hasan	*Why I Am a Muslim: An American Odyssey.* San Francisco: Thorsons Element, 2004.
Philip Hiro	*War Without End: The Rise of Islamist Terrorism and the Global Response.* New York: Routledge, 2002.
Samuel P. Huntington	*The Clash of Civilizations and the Remaking of World Order.* New York: Simon and Schuster, 1996.
Imam Khomeini	*Islam and Revolution: Writings and Declarations of Imam Khomeini.* Trans. H. Algar. Berkeley, CA: Mizan, 1981.
Bernard Lewis	*The Crisis of Islam: Holy War and Unholy Terror.* New York: Modern Library, 2003.
Bernard Lewis	*What Went Wrong? Western Impact and Middle Eastern Response.* New York: Oxford University Press, 2002.

Ahmed Rashid   *Taliban: Militant Islam, Oil, and Fundamentalism in Central Asia.* New Haven, CT: Yale University Press, 2000.

Edward Said   *Covering Islam: How the Media and Experts Determine How We See the Rest of the World.* New York: Vintage, 1997.

Lamia Rustum   *The Idea of Women in Fundamentalist Islam.* Miami:
Shehadeh   University of Florida Press, 2003.

Robert Spencer   *Islam Unveiled: Disturbing Questions About the World's Fastest-Growing Faith.* San Francisco: Encounter, 2002.

Ibn Warraq   *Why I Am Not a Muslim.* New York: Prometheus, 1995.

Ibn Warraq, ed.   *What the Quran Really Says.* New York: Prometheus, 2002.

Bat Yeor   *Islam and Dhimmitude: When Civilizations Collide.* Madison, NJ: Fairleigh Dickinson University Press, 2001.

Periodicals

Alain Besancon   "What Kind of Religion Is Islam?" *Commentary*, vol. 114, May 2004.

Roy Brown   "Opposing Political Islam," *Free Inquiry*, vol. 24, December 2003.

Christianity Today   "Competing Claims About Islam: Is It a Religion of Peace or of Violence?" October 2003.

Vincent Cornell   "A Muslim to Muslims: Reflections After September 11," *South Atlantic Quarterly*, vol. 101, no. 2, Spring 2002.

Peter David   "In the Name of Islam," *Economist*, September 13, 2003.

Khaled Abou El Fadl   "Terrorism Is at Odds with Islamic Tradition," *Los Angeles Times*, August 22, 2001.

Heba Raouf Ezzat   "Women and the Interpretation of Islamic Sources," *Women's Issues*, October 1999.

Reuven Firestone   "Religions Hold Mix of Justice and Mercy," *Jewish Journal of Greater Los Angeles*, January 2, 2004.

Thomas L. Friedman   "The Core of Muslim Rage," *New York Times*, March 6, 2002.

Sohail H. Hashmi   "The Qu'ran and Tolerance: An Interpretive Essay on Verse 5:48," *Journal of Human Rights*, January 2003.

Azam Kamguian   "Islam and the Liberation of Women in the Middle East," *Free Inquiry*, October/November 2003.

John Kelsay — "Osama bin Laden and the Just Conduct of War: Osama Appeals to the Traditions of Islam. Is He Right?" *America*, vol. 185, October 8, 2001.

David Klinghoffer — "Understanding the Stranger," *Publishers Weekly*, May 10, 2004.

Bernard Lewis — "License to Kill: Usama Bin Laden's Declaration of Jihad," *Foreign Affairs*, November/December 1998.

Ahmar Musatikhan — "The Roots of Islamic Extremism," *The World & I*, vol. 14, July 1999.

A. Rashid Omar — "Islam and Violence," *Ecumenical Review*, vol. 55, April 2003.

Daniel Pipes — "Jihad and the Professors," *Commentary*, vol. 114, November 2002.

James Piscatori — "The Turmoil Within," *Foreign Affairs*, May/June 2002.

David Pryce-Jones — "At War: Islam in Action: Extremism Now and Everywhere," *National Review*, vol. 53, December 3, 2001.

Salman Rushdie — "Yes, This Is About Islam," *New York Times*, November 2, 2001.

Jonathon Sacks — "The Dignity of Difference: Avoiding the Clash of Civilizations," *FPRI WIRE*, vol. 10, no. 3, July 2002.

Robert Spencer — "The War Is Over: The Jihad Isn't," FrontPageMagazine.com, August 18, 2003.

Teresa Watanabe — "Interpreting Islam: War and Peace," *Los Angeles Times*, October 5, 2001.

Index

Abu Bakr, 60
Adam, 52–53, 87
Ahmed, Akbar S., 8, 68
Alkhateeb, Sharifa, 10
Allah, nature of, 70–71
Amanpour, Christiane, 25
anti-Semitism, 35, 80
Aquinas, Thomas, 55
Arab lands, U.S. occupation of, 13–15
Arab world, diversity of, 19–20
Arafat, Yasir, 35

Bannerman, Patrick, 11
Bano, Afsar, 90
Battle of Tours, 34
Bhutto, Benazir, 9–10, 11
Bible, 45
bin Laden, Osama, 12, 20, 64
Brown, Widney, 9
Bush, George W., 8, 30, 67

Cairo Declaration, 87–88
capitalism, Islam is compatible with, 20–21
Charles (British prince), 10
Christian evangelists, 8
Christianity, is based on pacifism, 65–66
convivencia, 23–24
Crusades, 36, 66, 67
cultures, clash between Islamic and Western, 18–19, 24–25, 36

Dar al-Harb, 36, 38
Dar al-Islam, 36, 38
democracy, Islam and, 10
divorce, 9

Esposito, John L., 17
Eve, 87

Falwell, Jerry, 8
family, decline of, 94–95
fatwas, 15
Firestone, Reuven, 43
Flori, Jean, 63

God
  laws of, 52–53
  rejection of, 53–54
  see also Allah

Hashmi, Sohail H., 50
Haykal, Muhammad, 57–58
heaven
  entrance into, 47–48
  Muslim conception of, 45–47
holy war
  Islamic vs. Christian, 66–67
  see also jihad
homosexuality, 84–85
honor killings, 9
human nature, 52–54
humility, of Muhammad, 74–75
Huntington, Samuel P., 18–19

Iberian Peninsula, 23–24
Ibrahim, Anwar, 22–24
Imran, Samia, 9
Iran, relations between West and, 24–26
Iraq war, 67
Islam
  apologists for, 42
  clash of civilizations between West and, 18–19, 24–25, 36
  democratic principles and, 10
  dialogue between West and, 26–27
  diversity in, 28–29
  five pillars of, 71–72
  growth of, 8
  history of violence in, 64–65
  holy war on U.S. by, 12–16
  intolerance in, 9
  is compatible with capitalism, 20–21
  Islamic fundamentalism and, 39–40
  is peaceful religion, 9–10, 30–31
    con, 8–9, 32–36
  promotes terrorism, 37–42
    con, 43–49
  promotes universal humanity, 75–77
  strengthening of, 26–27
  totalitarianism of, 80–81
Islam and Capitalism (Rodinson), 20–21
Islamic empire, 77
Islamic fundamentalism
  Islam and, 39–40
  is violent, 40–41
  social justice and, 59
Islamic reformers

Abdurrahman Wahid, 22, 27–28
Anwar Ibrahim, 22–24
Mohammad Khatami, 22, 24–27
peaceful relations with West and,
   17–22
Israel, 35

Jesus, 65
Jews, hatred of, 35, 80
jihad, 38–39
   acquires military component,
      57–58
   declaration of, on U.S., 12–16
   history of, 34–35
   justifications for, 53–55, 58–59
   Muslim view of, 36
   as nonviolent resistance, 56–57
   rewards of, 39
   right conduct during, 60–61
   as tool for social justice, 59
   urged by Muhammad, 33, 34
   see also just war
Judaism, 44–45
just war, jihad is comparable to,
   50–62
   con, 63–67

Khaldun, Ibn, 51
Khamenei, Ayatollah Ali, 26
Khatami, Mohammad, 22, 24–27
Khomeini, Ayatollah, 15
Koran, 69–71
   contradictions in, 88–89
   Islamic fundamentalism and, 40
   violence in, 45
   on war, 38–39, 51–55, 60, 65
   on women, 10, 83–84, 86–89

Manji, Irshad, 78
Margolieth, D.S., 8–9
marriages, 76
Martel, Charles, 34
martyrdom, 47–48, 65–66
Marxism, 23
Medina, 57
Middle East, peace talks in, 35
motherhood, as main job of women,
   96
Mount Hira, 68–69
Muhammad
   call to Islam for, 69
   gentle nature of, 72–75, 77
   Meccan period of, 56–57
   political alliances of, 75–76
   on violence, 8–9, 47–48
   on war, 33, 34, 55–58, 65
multiculturalism, 41
Muqaddima (Ibn Khaldun), 51

Muslims
   diversity of, 19–20, 28–29
   growing number of, 8
   moderate, 64
   view of West by, 48–49, 67
Muslim scholars, self-proclaimed, 44,
   45
Muslim women
   are treated better than Western
      women, 90–98
   attire of, 10
   injustices against, 9, 79–89

Nahdatul Ulama (NU), 27
noncombatants, 47–48, 60–61
nonviolent resistance, 56–57

Ottoman Empire, 34–35

pacifism, 65–66
Piscatori, James, 20
pluralism, 23–24
Prophet. *See* Muhammad

Qur'an. *See* Koran
Qutb, Sayyid, 27, 41

rape victims, 9, 85–86, 88
reform movements, 21–22
   see also Islamic reformers
retaliation, law of, 56
Robertson, Pat, 32
Rodinson, Maxime, 20–21
Rushdie, Salman, 25

Sahih al-Bukhari, 47
Saudi Arabia, culture of, 19
September 11, 2001, 8, 12, 18, 30,
   63–64
social justice, 59
Spain, Muslim invaders in, 34
Spencer, Robert, 9
suicide bombers, 43, 47–48
Sunan al-Tirmidhi, 46, 48

terrorism, 8
   causes of, 18–19, 28
   has hijacked Islam, 43–49
   intellectual, 42
   Islam promotes, 37–42
Torah, 45
totalitarianism, 80–81
tribalism, 75–76

United States
   culture of, 19
   occupation of Arab lands by, 13–15
   relations between Iran and, 24–26

universal humanity, 75–77
Urban II (pope), 66

violence
    history of, in Islam, 8–9
    against Muslim women, 79–89
    promoted by Islam, 32–36

Wahid, Abdurrahman, 22, 27–28
war
    conceptions of, in Koran, 51–55,
        60, 65
    debates over grounds for, 58–59
    Muhammad's conception of, 33,
        34, 55–58, 65
    right conduct during, 60–61
    in spread of Islam, 34–35
    see also jihad; just war
war on terror, 67
Warraq, Ibn, 37

West
    clash of civilizations between Islam
        and, 18–19, 24–25, 36
    decadence of, 93–94
    decline of family in, 94–95
    dialogue between Islam and, 26–27
    Muslim perception of, 48–49, 67
    peaceful relations between Islam
        and, 17–29
    relations between Iran and, 24–26
    see also United States
Western values, 41–42, 59
women
    Muhammad's kindness to, 73–74
    rights of, in Koran, 10, 86–89
    see also Muslim women
women's liberation movement,
    92–93

Zeinab, Evelyn, 10